GREAT FOOD FAST

FROM THE KITCHENS OF MARTHA STEWART LIVING

Clarkson Potter | Publishers
New York

Copyright © 2007 by Martha Stewart Living Omnimedia, Inc.

All rights reserved.

Published in the United States by Clarkson Potter/Publishers,
an imprint of the Crown Publishing Group, a division of Random
House, Inc., New York.

www.crownpublishing.com
www.clarksonpotter.com

Clarkson N. Potter is a trademark and Potter and colophon
are registered trademarks of Random House, Inc.

The recipes in the book originally appeared in issues
of EVERYDAY FOOD magazine.

Library of Congress Cataloging-in-Publication Data
is available by request.

ISBN 978-0-307-35416-7

Printed in the United States of America

Design by William van Roden
Photograph credits appear on page 374.

10 9 8 7 6 5 4 3 2 1

First Edition

To home cooks everywhere, for recognizing the
importance and pleasure of each meal

CONTENTS

183 FALL

BASICS 345

REFERENCE 364

INTRODUCTION

Ever since the launch of *Everyday Food* magazine in early 2003, I have wanted to gather our fastest, easiest, most delicious recipes in one convenient place. I am delighted that you now hold this wonderful book in your hands.

As I wrote in my letter in the magazine's first issue, "our goal is to teach you how to keep it simple (but never at the expense of taste) and to help you spend less time in the kitchen and more time with your family." In fact, it was my own mother, Martha Kostyra, who provided the inspiration for *Everyday Food*. When I was growing up, she prepared daily meals for our family of eight. Mom knew how to feed a large group with a minimum of fuss and waste, with an emphasis on wholesome foods, simply prepared. We never ate so-called convenience foods.

In creating *Everyday Food,* we wanted to help people return to this more healthful, enjoyable way of cooking and eating—and to do so without spending hours in the kitchen. We suspected this approach would be popular, and have been so gratified by the positive response to our little publication. In fact, *Everyday Food* is not so "little" anymore—it has an impressive circulation and continues to grow. In early 2005, we launched the companion television series on PBS, and that, too, reaches a wide audience of loyal fans who write and tell us they are grateful to have so many accessible recipes to try and to share.

Most of the recipes in this book were chosen for their ease of preparation. When you see a recipe that says "prep time 25 minutes," you can be assured that you won't spend longer than that getting the dish ready. Our recipe developers and testers work hard to give time estimates that are manageable for every cook, regardless of skill or expertise. They also create recipes using supermarket ingredients—not specialty items. That means you can shop once on the weekend and make satisfying meals all week long, or stop at the store on the way home from work to pick up ingredients for a great dinner.

You'll notice that we divided the recipes here by season. This is because we tend to use different cooking techniques at different times of year—grilling in the summer, for example, and roasting in the winter—and I know that I crave different flavors depending on the season too. But because the ingredients are so readily available, you can really try any recipe on almost any day. I do hope that you turn to this book every night of the week and that it becomes your most trusted kitchen companion in the kitchen.

Martha Stewart

SPRING

WHEN THE WEATHER CHANGES, your style of cooking does, too. In spring-time, as we emerge from the long, often dark winter months, we yearn for simple, uncomplicated dishes, with a healthy dose of market-fresh vegetables.

Here are recipes that fulfill the wish for relaxed preparations, such as no-fuss, toss-and-serve pastas; others, including chops cooked in a flash, minimize time spent at the stove; still others require nothing more than a quick assembly of ingredients, such as main-course salads topped with turkey, steak, or salmon. Here, too, are variations on spring vegetables, including asparagus, which is blended into a creamy soup, roasted and served as a side dish, and paired with Gruyère cheese in a simple but elegant tart made with store-bought puff pastry.

Desserts comply with these same seasonal yearnings. Rhubarb crisp tastes of spring but takes only 15 minutes to prepare; strawberry short-cake, another perennial favorite, requires just 30 minutes. Take advantage of the pleasant shift in temperature—the goal is to spend less time in the kitchen and more time outside, enjoying the wonders of spring.

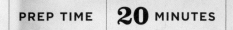

FREEZING THE SOUP

Omit the cream and lemon juice. Cool to
room temperature before dividing among
airtight containers (leaving 1 inch of
space at top). Freeze for up to 2 months.
Defrost overnight in the refrigerator;
reheat over low heat. Stir in the cream
and lemon juice before serving.

Add a slice of toast topped with melted cheese, and you have a light dinner or lunch. This recipe makes enough soup for eight people, but you can easily freeze the leftovers if serving fewer (directions for freezing are opposite).

CREAM OF ASPARAGUS SOUP

SERVES 8 ■ PREP TIME: 20 MINUTES ■ TOTAL TIME: 30 MINUTES

3 tablespoons butter

1½ cups coarsely chopped shallots (about 6 large)

½ teaspoon dried thyme

3 tablespoons all-purpose flour

3 pounds asparagus, trimmed and cut into 1-inch pieces

Coarse salt

⅓ cup heavy cream

2 to 3 tablespoons fresh lemon juice

1 In a large (4-quart) saucepan, melt the butter over medium heat. Add the shallots and thyme; cook until the shallots are soft, about 5 minutes. Add the flour; cook until incorporated, stirring constantly, about 1 minute.

2 Add the asparagus and 6 cups water; season generously with salt. Cover, and bring to a boil. Reduce heat; cover, and simmer, until the asparagus is bright green and just tender, 2 to 4 minutes.

3 Working in batches, purée the soup in a blender until very smooth. To prevent splattering, fill the blender only halfway, and allow heat to escape: Remove the cap from the hole in the lid, and cover the lid with a dish towel. (To freeze, see note, opposite.) If serving right away, stir in the cream and lemon juice.

To serve this Mexican mainstay, ladle the hot soup into bowls, and then let everyone pick and choose from among the suggested garnishes.

TORTILLA SOUP

SERVES 4 ■ PREP TIME: 30 MINUTES ■ **TOTAL TIME: 30 MINUTES**

For the soup
- 4 skinless chicken thighs (about 1½ pounds)
- 1 can (14.5 ounces) reduced-sodium chicken broth
- 1 jalapeño chile, diced (with seeds for more heat)
- 6 corn tortillas (6-inch)
- 3 tablespoons canola oil
  Coarse salt

For the garnish
- 1 cup shredded Monterey Jack cheese (5 ounces)
- 4 large scallions, thinly sliced (about ½ cup)
- 1 green bell pepper, ribs and seeds removed, diced
- 1 avocado, peeled, pitted, and diced
- ¼ cup cilantro sprigs
- 1 lime, cut in wedges

1 Preheat the oven to 400°F. In a large pot, bring the chicken, broth, jalapeño, and 8 cups of water to a boil over medium-high heat. Reduce the heat to medium; simmer until the chicken is cooked through, about 15 minutes. Transfer the chicken to a plate; let cool.

2 Brush both sides of the tortillas with oil, stacking them as you go. Cut the stack in half, and then slice crosswise into ½-inch strips. Place the strips on a rimmed baking sheet; bake, tossing the strips occasionally, until golden, 15 to 20 minutes.

3 Using a large spoon, skim the fat from the surface of the broth in the pot, and strain the liquid through a sieve into a clean pot (you should have about 8 cups). Shred the chicken with a fork or with your fingers, and return it to the pot. Stir in 1 teaspoon salt. Divide the soup among serving bowls, and add the tortilla strips. Garnish as desired.

PLANNING AHEAD
The chicken can be cooked up to a day in advance; cool, then store the chicken and cooking liquid separately in the refrigerator. Shred the meat just before using. You can also use leftover or store-bought roasted chicken in this soup; use two quarts homemade or reduced-sodium canned chicken broth instead of the cooking liquid.

In this recipe for a popular Chinese dish, an egg is stirred into the simmering soup to form tiny ribbons. For more flavor, add a teaspoon of toasted sesame oil just before serving.

HOT AND SOUR SOUP

SERVES 4 ■ PREP TIME: 20 MINUTES ■ TOTAL TIME: 20 MINUTES

2 cans (14.5 ounces each) reduced-sodium chicken broth

2 tablespoons soy sauce

¼ to ½ teaspoon red pepper flakes

8 ounces fresh shiitake mushrooms, stemmed, caps thinly sliced (about 4 cups)

3 to 4 tablespoons rice vinegar

2 tablespoons cornstarch

1 large egg, lightly beaten

½ package (7 ounces) soft or firm tofu, cut into ¼-inch cubes, drained well

2 tablespoons finely grated peeled fresh ginger

3 scallions, thinly sliced

1 In a large (5-quart) pot, combine the broth, soy sauce, red pepper flakes, and 2 cups water. Bring to a boil over medium heat. Add the mushrooms; reduce the heat, and simmer until tender, about 10 minutes.

2 In a small bowl, whisk together 3 tablespoons of the vinegar and the cornstarch. Add to the pot; simmer, stirring, until the soup is thickened, about 1 minute.

3 Add the egg through a slotted spoon, and stir to form ribbons. Stir in the tofu. Remove from the heat; let stand, covered, for 1 minute. Put the ginger in a small sieve, and squeeze to release its juice into the soup (discard the solids). Taste; add the remaining tablespoon vinegar, if desired. Serve sprinkled with the scallions.

PREPARING TOFU
Be sure to drain the tofu thoroughly before adding it to the soup so it will soak up the flavor of the broth.

PREP TIME | **15** MINUTES

Depending on the weather, serve this comforting soup hot or cold. You can quickly chill it by placing it into a metal bowl set into an ice bath; stir frequently until the soup reaches the desired temperature.

POTATO-LEEK SOUP

SERVES 4 ■ PREP TIME: 15 MINUTES ■ TOTAL TIME: 45 MINUTES

- 6 medium leeks (about 2¼ pounds), whites only, halved lengthwise and thinly sliced crosswise, cleaned
- 2 cans (14.5 ounces each) reduced-sodium chicken broth
- 1 baking potato (8 ounces), peeled and diced
  Coarse salt
- ¾ cup heavy cream
- ½ cup snipped fresh chives

1 In a large saucepan, combine the leeks, broth, potato, 2 cups water, and 1 teaspoon salt. Bring to a boil; reduce the heat to medium-low, and simmer until the vegetables are very tender, 20 to 25 minutes.

2 Working in batches, purée the soup in a blender, transferring it to a clean bowl as you work. (To prevent splattering, fill the blender only halfway, and allow heat to escape: Remove the cap from the hole in the lid, and cover the lid firmly with a dish towel.) Stir the cream into the puréed soup, and season with salt. Garnish with the chives. Serve immediately.

3 If desired, chill the soup: Cover loosely with plastic wrap, and chill until cold, at least 2 hours and up to 2 days. If necessary, thin with water, and season with salt. Serve the soup in chilled glasses, garnished with chives.

WASHING LEEKS
Leeks can be extremely dirty and are best cleaned after they've been trimmed and cut. Soak cut leeks in a bowl of cool water; lift them out, replace the water, and repeat until no grit remains at the bottom of bowl. Drain on paper towels.

This salad works best with baby spinach; if you want to substitute regular spinach, tear it into small pieces before tossing with other ingredients. You can use tart or sweet cherries.

SPINACH SALAD WITH DRIED CHERRIES

SERVES 4
PREP TIME: 10 MINUTES
TOTAL TIME: 10 MINUTES

- ¼ cup raw green pumpkin seeds
- 4 teaspoons red-wine vinegar
- 1 tablespoon Dijon mustard
- 2 tablespoons olive oil
  Coarse salt and fresh ground pepper
- 8 ounces baby spinach
- ½ cup thinly sliced red onion
- ½ cup dried cherries

1 Preheat the oven to 350°F. Spread the pumpkin seeds in a single layer in a pie plate; bake until puffed and brown, about 10 minutes.

2 Meanwhile, in a large bowl, whisk together the vinegar, mustard, and oil until combined and thickened; season with salt and pepper.

3 Add the spinach, onion, and cherries to the dressing; toss to combine. Top the salad with the pumpkin seeds and serve immediately.

PREP TIME **10** MINUTES

From the Friuli region of Italy, the Parmesan wafers known as frico add a crisp and salty counterpoint to the salad.

LEAF-LETTUCE SALAD WITH PARMESAN CRISPS

SERVES 6 ▪ PREP TIME: 30 MINUTES ▪ TOTAL TIME: 30 MINUTES

½ cup finely grated Parmesan cheese (2 ounces)

¾ pound red or green leaf lettuce

Reduced-Fat Herb Vinaigrette (recipe below)

Coarse salt and fresh ground pepper

1 Preheat the oven to 350°F. Divide the cheese into four mounds on a parchment-lined baking sheet, at least 4 inches apart. With the back of a spoon, spread each mound into an even 4-inch round.

2 Bake until melted and golden brown, about 10 minutes, rotating the sheet halfway through. With a thin metal spatula, transfer the crisps to a wire rack; let cool.

3 Tear the lettuce leaves into bite-size pieces (about 12 cups). Toss with the vinaigrette; season with salt and pepper. Serve the salad with the Parmesan crisps.

REDUCED-FAT HERB VINAIGRETTE

1 tablespoon fresh lemon juice

2 teaspoons Dijon mustard

¼ cup firmly packed fresh herbs (such as basil, cilantro, or parsley)

½ small garlic clove

Coarse salt and fresh ground pepper

3 tablespoons extra-virgin olive oil

In a blender, combine the lemon juice, mustard, herbs, garlic, and ¼ cup cold water; season with salt and pepper. Purée until smooth. With the motor running, add the olive oil in a steady stream until emulsified.

Wait until you are ready to serve the salad before dressing it. Lavash is sold in most supermarkets; if you can't find it, a large pita works just as well.

GREEK SALAD WITH SEASONED FLATBREAD

SERVES 4 ■ PREP TIME: 20 MINUTES ■ **TOTAL TIME: 20 MINUTES**

3 tablespoons olive oil

3 tablespoons red-wine vinegar

1 teaspoon minced garlic

Coarse salt and fresh ground pepper

1 head romaine lettuce, cut into bite-size pieces

1 pint cherry or grape tomatoes, halved

1½ cups crumbled feta cheese (8 ounces)

½ medium red onion, halved and thinly sliced

1 large cucumber, peeled, halved, and thinly sliced

½ cup kalamata olives, pitted

Seasoned Flatbread (recipe below)

In a large bowl, whisk the oil with the vinegar and garlic; season with salt and pepper. Add the remaining ingredients and toss. Serve the salad with the seasoned flatbread.

SEASONED FLATBREAD

2 pieces lavash (or large pita bread, split in half)

1 tablespoon olive oil

2 teaspoons red-wine vinegar

½ teaspoon finely grated lemon zest

1 garlic clove, minced

1 teaspoon dried oregano

Coarse salt and fresh ground pepper

Preheat the oven to 400°F. Line a baking sheet with parchment; place the lavash on top. In a small bowl, whisk together the olive oil, vinegar, lemon zest, and garlic. Brush the mixture evenly over the lavash; sprinkle with the oregano. Season with salt and pepper. Bake until golden and crisp, 5 to 10 minutes. Break in half, and serve. **SERVES 4**

PREP TIME | **20** MINUTES

This recipe is based on a popular bistro salad. The goat cheese disks can be prepared through step two up to a day ahead. Cover with plastic wrap, and keep in the refrigerator. Brush the disks with olive oil just before broiling.

CRISP GOAT-CHEESE SALAD

SERVES 4 ■ PREP TIME: 30 MINUTES ■ **TOTAL TIME: 30 MINUTES**

½ cup olive oil,
   plus more for baking sheet

3 large red potatoes
   (about 1 pound)

1 large egg
   Coarse salt and
   fresh ground pepper

1½ cups plain breadcrumbs

1 log fresh goat cheese
   (12 ounces)

1 tablespoon white-wine vinegar

1 tablespoon grainy or
   Dijon mustard

8 ounces mesclun or mixed
   salad greens

1 Heat the broiler. Brush a baking sheet with oil; set aside. Place the potatoes in a medium saucepan, cover with cold water, and bring to a boil. Simmer just until fork-tender, 20 to 25 minutes. Rinse the potatoes under cold water until cool enough to handle, and cut into 1-inch chunks.

2 In a shallow bowl, whisk the egg with ¼ teaspoon each salt and pepper. Place the breadcrumbs in another shallow bowl. Slice the goat cheese into 8 rounds (see note below), and pat each into a disk about ½ inch thick. Dip the disks in the egg and then in the breadcrumbs, coating evenly. Place on the prepared baking sheet.

3 In a large bowl, whisk together the vinegar, mustard, and ¼ teaspoon each salt and pepper. Slowly add ¼ cup of the oil, whisking to emulsify. Set aside.

4 Brush the disks lightly with the remaining ¼ cup oil, and broil until golden and crisp, about 5 minutes.

5 Toss the greens and potatoes in the dressing. Divide the salad among 4 plates, and top each with 2 cheese disks.

SLICING GOAT CHEESE
Freezing the goat-cheese log for several minutes makes it easier to slice.

This classic French sauce also makes an excellent topping for fish, such as seared salmon or trout. For four servings, steam 1½ pounds trimmed asparagus until crisp-tender, toss with butter, and season with salt and pepper, as desired.

SAUTÉED CHICKEN IN MUSTARD-CREAM SAUCE

SERVES 4 ■ PREP TIME: 20 MINUTES ■ **TOTAL TIME: 20 MINUTES**

4 boneless, skinless chicken breast halves (6 ounces each)

Coarse salt and fresh ground pepper

2 tablespoons olive oil

¼ cup dry white wine or chicken broth

½ cup heavy cream

2 tablespoons Dijon mustard

1 teaspoon dried tarragon (or 1 tablespoon chopped fresh)

1 Sprinkle each chicken breast with ¼ teaspoon each salt and pepper. In a large skillet, heat the olive oil over medium-high heat. Add the chicken; sauté until cooked through, 10 to 12 minutes, turning once. Transfer to a plate; keep warm.

2 Pour the wine into the hot skillet; cook, stirring, until reduced by half, about 1 minute. Whisk in the cream, mustard, and tarragon. Cook, whisking, until thickened, about 2 minutes.

3 Pour any accumulated chicken juices into the sauce. Right before serving, drizzle the cream sauce over the sautéed chicken.

PREP TIME | **20** MINUTES

Served with Carrot-Cumin Slaw (recipe below) or potato salad, this chicken dinner is perfect picnic fare. Leftover chicken makes a great lunch the next day.

BUTTERMILK BAKED CHICKEN

SERVES 4 ■ PREP TIME: 10 MINUTES ■ TOTAL TIME: 50 MINUTES

Vegetable oil, for baking sheet
8 slices white bread
1 cup buttermilk
1 teaspoon hot-pepper sauce
Coarse salt and
fresh ground pepper
¾ cup grated Parmesan cheese
(2½ ounces)
1 teaspoon dried thyme
4 pounds chicken parts
(preferably legs, thighs, and
wings), rinsed and patted dry

1 Preheat the oven to 400°F. Generously rub a baking sheet with oil. In a food processor, pulse the bread until it turns into coarse crumbs.

2 In a large bowl, stir together the buttermilk, hot-pepper sauce, ¾ teaspoon salt, and ½ teaspoon pepper. In a separate bowl, mix the breadcrumbs, Parmesan, thyme, and ⅛ teaspoon pepper.

3 Place the chicken in the buttermilk mixture, turning to coat evenly. Working with one piece at a time, remove the chicken from the liquid, letting the excess drip back into the bowl; dredge in the breadcrumb mixture, turning to coat evenly. Place the coated chicken pieces on the prepared baking sheet. Leave enough space between the chicken pieces so that they crisp evenly all the way around.

4 Bake until the chicken is golden brown, about 35 minutes.

CARROT-CUMIN SLAW

¼ head green cabbage, shredded
3 carrots, coarsely grated
1 jalapeño chile,
seeded and minced
¼ cup canola oil
2 tablespoons fresh lime
(or lemon) juice
3 tablespoons chopped fresh
cilantro or parsley
½ teaspoon ground cumin
Coarse salt and
fresh ground pepper

In a large bowl, combine the cabbage, carrots, and jalapeño. Drizzle the mixture with the canola oil and lime juice; sprinkle with the cilantro, cumin, ¼ teaspoon salt, and ⅛ teaspoon pepper. Toss well.
SERVES 4

You can mix and match the listed ingredients to create your own version of this main-course salad. We used store-bought roasted turkey, but chicken also works well.

TURKEY COBB SALAD

SERVES 4 ■ PREP TIME: 20 MINUTES ■ **TOTAL TIME: 20 MINUTES**

4 slices bacon (4 ounces)

3 tablespoons red-wine vinegar

2 tablespoons olive oil

1 teaspoon Dijon mustard

1 large head romaine lettuce, shredded

8 ounces roasted turkey breast, cut into ¾-inch dice (2 cups)

½ ripe avocado, pitted, peeled, and cut into ½-inch dice

3 ounces blue cheese, crumbled (¾ cup)

2 hard-cooked eggs, cut into ¼-inch dice

2 plum tomatoes, cut into ½-inch dice

Coarse salt and fresh ground pepper

1 In a 10-inch skillet, cook the bacon over medium heat until crisp on both sides, 3 to 5 minutes. Transfer to a paper-towel-lined plate to drain. Let cool, then crumble the bacon.

2 In a small bowl, whisk together the vinegar, oil, and mustard. Place the lettuce on a serving platter, and toss with the dressing. Arrange the remaining ingredients on the lettuce as desired, and season with salt and pepper.

SHREDDING LETTUCE
Discard the tough outer leaves, and cut the head in half lengthwise. With the cut sides down, thinly slice the halves crosswise until you reach the core.

A crisp salad dressed with oil, vinegar, and herbs is a light alternative to a side of pasta. The chicken makes wonderful leftovers. Reheat it for 10 minutes, and try it in a sandwich with a little extra sauce on the side.

•

CHICKEN PARMIGIANA

SERVES 4 ■ PREP TIME: 30 MINUTES ■ **TOTAL TIME: 30 MINUTES**

¾ cup plain breadcrumbs

¾ cup grated Parmesan cheese

8 chicken cutlets or 4 boneless, skinless chicken breast halves, halved horizontally (about 1 ½ pounds total)

Coarse salt and fresh ground pepper

1 large egg, lightly beaten

2 cups Easy Chunky Tomato Sauce (page 356) or jarred tomato sauce

¼ cup olive oil

6 ounces mozzarella cheese, preferably fresh, cut into eight ¼-inch-thick slices

1 Heat the broiler. Combine the breadcrumbs and Parmesan in a shallow bowl. Season both sides of the chicken with ½ teaspoon salt and ¼ teaspoon pepper. Dip the chicken in the beaten egg, then dredge in the breadcrumb mixture, turning to coat both sides.

2 Spread the tomato sauce onto the bottom of a 10-by-15-inch baking dish. Heat 2 tablespoons of the oil in a large nonstick skillet over medium heat. Place 4 chicken cutlets in the skillet; cook until golden, 1 to 2 minutes on each side. Using a spatula, transfer the browned chicken cutlets to the baking dish, placing them on top of the sauce. Repeat with the remaining oil and chicken cutlets.

3 Top each cutlet with a slice of mozzarella. Broil about 4 inches from the heat source until the sauce is hot and the cheese is melted and lightly browned in spots, 5 to 8 minutes. Serve immediately.

DREDGING CHICKEN
Use shallow bowls for the egg and the coating mixture. After dipping the chicken in the egg, let the excess egg drip off before coating the cutlet in the breadcrumb mixture.

Look for hoisin sauce and rice vinegar in the Asian foods section of your supermarket. Although ingredients vary, hoisin is generally made with soybeans, chiles, and spices. It's used as a seasoning at the table and in cooking.

CASHEW CHICKEN

SERVES 4 ■ PREP TIME: 30 MINUTES ■ **TOTAL TIME: 30 MINUTES**

1½ pounds boneless, skinless
    chicken breast,
    cut into 1-inch cubes

1 tablespoon cornstarch
    Coarse salt and
    fresh ground pepper

2 tablespoons vegetable oil

6 garlic cloves, minced

8 scallions, white and green
    parts separated,
    each cut into 1-inch pieces

2 tablespoons rice vinegar

3 tablespoons hoisin sauce

¾ cup raw cashews (4 ounces),
    toasted (see note below)
    White rice, for serving (optional)

1 In a medium bowl, toss the chicken with the cornstarch until the chicken is coated; season with ¾ teaspoon salt and ¼ teaspoon pepper.

2 In a large nonstick skillet, heat 1 tablespoon of the oil over medium-high heat. Cook half the chicken, tossing often, until browned, about 3 minutes. Transfer to a plate.

3 Add the remaining oil and chicken to the skillet along with the garlic and the white parts of the scallions. Cook, tossing often, until the chicken is browned, about 3 minutes. Return the first batch of chicken to the pan. Add the vinegar; cook until evaporated, about 30 seconds.

4 Add the hoisin sauce and ¼ cup water; cook, tossing, until the chicken is cooked through, about 1 minute. Remove from the heat. Stir in the scallion greens and cashews. Serve immediately over white rice, if desired.

TOASTING CASHEWS
Spread the cashews on a baking sheet, and toast in a 350°F oven until golden and fragrant, about 10 minutes.

PREP TIME **30** MINUTES

STUFFING THE CHICKEN
Using a sharp paring knife, make a horizontal incision in each chicken breast, creating a pocket. Be careful not to slice all the way through.

The addition of goat cheese, apricots, and pesto lends a Mediterranean flavor to chicken. The pesto is made with fresh mint and almonds, rather than the usual basil and pine nuts.

ALMOND-APRICOT CHICKEN WITH MINT PESTO

SERVES 4 ■ PREP TIME: 30 MINUTES ■ **TOTAL TIME: 50 MINUTES**

4 boneless, skinless chicken breast halves (6 ounces each)

½ cup sliced almonds

2 ounces goat cheese

4 dried apricots, cut into ¼-inch pieces (3 tablespoons)

Coarse salt and fresh ground pepper

⅓ cup plain breadcrumbs

1 large egg, lightly beaten

1 tablespoon olive oil

Mint Pesto (recipe below)

1 Preheat the oven to 375°F. Cut a slit in one side of each chicken breast to create a pocket about 4 inches long.

2 In a small bowl, combine ¼ cup of the almonds with the goat cheese and apricots. Stuff each breast with one quarter of the mixture. Season with ½ teaspoon salt and ¼ teaspoon pepper.

3 On a plate, combine the breadcrumbs and the remaining ¼ cup almonds. Dip each breast into the beaten egg, then dredge in the breadcrumb mixture.

4 Heat the oil in a large ovenproof non-stick skillet over medium heat. Cook the chicken until golden, 3 to 4 minutes on each side. Transfer to the oven; bake until cooked through, about 15 minutes. Serve hot with the mint pesto on the side.

MINT PESTO

3 cups lightly packed fresh mint

¼ cup sliced almonds

½ cup extra-virgin olive oil

Coarse salt

1 In a food processor, combine the mint and almonds; process until finely chopped.

2 With the motor running, gradually pour the olive oil through the feed tube. Season with salt. Keep at room temperature until ready to serve. Store leftover pesto in a sealed container in the refrigerator for up to two weeks; let it come to room temperature before serving.

This recipe is based on a Mexican dish created to use up leftovers. For an authentic touch, use fresh Mexican cheese (*queso fresco*) or aged (*queso añejo*) in place of feta. Look for both in specialty food stores and Mexican markets.

CHICKEN CHILAQUILES

SERVES 4 ■ PREP TIME: 30 MINUTES ■ TOTAL TIME: 30 MINUTES

1 tablespoon olive oil

4 garlic cloves, chopped

1 can (28 ounces) whole peeled tomatoes in purée

2 chipotle chiles in adobo (from a small can), finely chopped (about 1 heaping tablespoon), plus 1 tablespoon adobo sauce (from same can)

Coarse salt

1 small roasted chicken (about 1 ¾ pounds; recipe, page 351) or cooked rotisserie chicken, skinned and shredded (about 4 cups), carcass discarded

½ cup lightly packed cilantro leaves, chopped, plus additional sprigs for garnish

4 cups (about 3 ounces) tortilla chips

¼ cup reduced-fat sour cream

¼ cup crumbled feta cheese (about 2 ounces)

1 Combine the oil and garlic in a large (3- to 4-quart) saucepan. Cook over medium heat, stirring occasionally, until the garlic is fragrant and sizzling, 1 to 2 minutes.

2 Add the tomatoes with their purée (breaking tomatoes up), chipotles and adobo sauce, and 1 cup water. Bring to a boil; season with salt. Reduce the heat and simmer rapidly until lightly thickened, 6 to 8 minutes.

3 Add the chicken and cook, stirring, until hot, about 1 minute. Remove from the heat; stir in the chopped cilantro.

4 Divide the chips among 4 shallow bowls; top with the chicken mixture and sauce. Garnish with cilantro sprigs, sour cream, and feta. Serve.

PREP TIME | **30** MINUTES

We like this steak served with sauteed mushrooms and polenta, but it would also be great with a green salad or Parmesan Steak Fries (page 83). And since it's made with commonly available ingredients, you can enjoy it year-round.

STEAK WITH PARSLEY SAUCE AND SAUTÉED MUSHROOMS

SERVES 4 ■ PREP TIME: 10 MINUTES ■ **TOTAL TIME: 25 MINUTES**

2 strip, shell, or sirloin steaks (about ¾ pound each and 1 inch thick)

2 teaspoons olive oil

Coarse salt and fresh ground pepper

Parsley Sauce (recipe below)

Sautéed Mushrooms (recipe below)

1 Coat the steaks with the olive oil; season with salt and pepper.

2 Heat a large nonstick skillet over medium-high. Add the steaks; cook until browned, 5 to 6 minutes per side for medium-rare.

3 Transfer the steaks to a cutting board; let rest 10 minutes before slicing thin. Serve with the parsley sauce and sautéed mushrooms.

PARSLEY SAUCE

1 garlic clove, chopped

1 cup loosely packed fresh parsley leaves

¼ cup olive oil

Coarse salt and fresh ground pepper

In a blender, purée the garlic, parsley, olive oil, and 3 tablespoons water until smooth. Season with salt and pepper. This recipe makes a generous amount of sauce. Any leftover sauce can be stored in the refrigerator, covered in an airtight container, for up to 3 days. **MAKES ½ CUP**

SAUTÉED MUSHROOMS

6 ounces shiitake mushrooms

8 ounces cremini mushrooms (also called baby portobellos)

2 teaspoons olive oil

1 shallot, minced

Coarse salt and fresh ground pepper

Cut off the shiitake mushroom stems and discard; thinly slice the caps. Trim the tough ends of the cremini mushrooms, then quarter each mushroom. Heat the olive oil in a large nonstick skillet over medium-high heat. Add the shallot; cook until lightly browned, 1 to 2 minutes. Add the cremini; cook, stirring occasionally, until softened, about 5 minutes. Reduce the heat to medium. Add the shiitakes; cook until tender, 5 to 7 minutes. Season with salt and pepper. **SERVES 4**

PREP TIME **10** MINUTES

BASIC POLENTA
Recipe, page 360

Radish and avocado are traditional Mexican toppings for tacos. Here they are combined in a salsa that can be served with tacos or as an appetizer with tortilla chips.

BEEF TACOS WITH RADISH AND AVOCADO SALSA

SERVES 4 ■ PREP TIME: 15 MINUTES ■ TOTAL TIME: 25 MINUTES

1 avocado, halved, pitted, peeled, and cut into ¾-inch cubes

6 large red radishes, ends trimmed, halved, thinly sliced

¼ cup chopped cilantro

1 tablespoon chopped pickled jalapeño chile

2 teaspoons fresh lime juice, plus 1 lime cut into 8 wedges, for garnish (optional)

1 teaspoon olive oil

Coarse salt and fresh ground pepper

1 pound skirt steak, cut crosswise into 3 pieces

1 tablespoon ground cumin

8 corn tortillas (6-inch)

1 Heat the broiler, with the rack 4 inches from the heat. Line a rimmed baking sheet with aluminum foil. In a bowl, gently stir together the avocado, radishes, cilantro, jalapeño, lime juice, and oil; season with salt. Cover with plastic wrap, pressing it directly against the surface of the salsa (to prevent discoloring); set aside.

2 Arrange the steak on the baking sheet. Rub both sides with cumin; season generously with salt and pepper. Broil without turning until well browned, 6 to 8 minutes for medium-rare. Transfer the steak to a cutting board; tent with foil, and let rest for 5 minutes.

3 While the steak is broiling, stack and wrap the tortillas in a dampened kitchen towel; microwave until hot and pliable, 1 to 2 minutes. (Alternatively, wrap in foil, and warm in the lower third of the oven, 5 minutes.)

4 Cut the steak crosswise into 2-inch-wide pieces; slice thin on the diagonal. Dividing evenly, place the beef on the tortillas; top with the salsa. Serve with lime wedges.

This hearty salad contains many ingredients and flavorings commonly found in Thai cuisine, including lime juice, chile pepper, mint, bean sprouts, and peanuts.

THAI-STYLE STEAK SALAD

SERVES 4 ■ PREP TIME: 30 MINUTES ■ **TOTAL TIME: 40 MINUTES**

¼ cup fresh lime juice

1 tablespoon soy sauce

1 tablespoon sugar

¼ to ½ teaspoon red pepper flakes

3 tablespoons vegetable oil

2 boneless rib-eye steaks
(each 8 ounces and ¾ inch thick)
Coarse salt and
fresh ground pepper

½ pound carrots (3 to 4 medium)

1 medium head romaine lettuce,
cut crosswise into 1-inch ribbons

½ cup fresh mint leaves

1 cup fresh bean sprouts (optional)

⅓ cup salted peanuts, chopped
(optional)

1 Make marinade: In a medium bowl or liquid measuring cup, whisk together the lime juice, soy sauce, sugar, red pepper flakes, and oil. Season the steaks generously with salt and pepper; place in a baking dish. Pour one quarter of the marinade over the steaks (reserve the remaining marinade); turn the steaks to coat. Let the steaks marinate up to 30 minutes.

2 In a large skillet, cook the steaks on medium-high heat, turning once, 2 to 3 minutes per side for medium-rare. Transfer to a cutting board; tent loosely with aluminum foil, and let rest, 5 to 10 minutes. Slice the steaks across the grain into ¼-inch-thick slices; halve the slices crosswise. Transfer to a large bowl, and toss with the reserved marinade.

3 With a vegetable peeler, cut the carrots into long ribbons (see photo below). Add to the steak in the bowl, along with the lettuce and mint; toss to combine. Divide the salad among 4 shallow bowls. Sprinkle with the bean sprouts and peanuts, if desired.

WARM WHITE BEAN SALAD
Recipe, page 85

The rhubarb sauce can be refrigerated in an airtight container for up to 1 week. Try it with chicken or drizzled over toasted bread or crackers topped with goat cheese. The cherries can be replaced with other dried fruit, such as golden raisins.

PORK CHOPS WITH RHUBARB-CHERRY SAUCE

SERVES 4 ▪ PREP TIME: 30 MINUTES ▪ **TOTAL TIME: 45 MINUTES**

½ cup dried cherries

1 tablespoon balsamic vinegar

¼ cup hot water

1 teaspoon plus 2 tablespoons olive oil

½ cup finely chopped onion

8 to 10 ounces rhubarb, ends trimmed, cut crosswise into ½-inch pieces (2 cups)

3 tablespoons sugar

Pinch of ground nutmeg

Coarse salt and fresh ground pepper

4 pork loin chops (each ½ inch thick and 6 to 8 ounces)

1 In a small bowl, combine the cherries with the vinegar and hot water; let stand 10 minutes to soften.

2 Meanwhile, in a small saucepan, heat 1 teaspoon oil over medium-low heat. Add the onion; cook until softened, stirring occasionally, about 10 minutes.

3 To the saucepan, add the cherry mixture, rhubarb, and sugar; bring to a boil. Reduce the heat; simmer until the rhubarb has softened, 5 to 8 minutes. Stir in the nutmeg; season with salt and pepper. Remove from the heat; keep warm.

4 Generously season both sides of the pork chops with salt and pepper. In a large skillet, heat the remaining 2 tablespoons oil over medium-high heat. Cook the pork (in two batches, if necessary, to avoid crowding the pan) until browned and cooked through, 3 to 4 minutes per side. Serve topped with the warm sauce.

SNAP PEAS WITH MINT

1 tablespoon butter

1 pound trimmed snap peas

½ cup (packed) thinly sliced fresh mint leaves

Coarse salt and fresh ground pepper

In a 12-inch nonstick skillet, bring 1 cup water and the butter to a boil over high heat. Add the snap peas; cover, and cook until bright green, about 2 minutes. Remove the lid; reduce the heat to medium. Continue cooking, tossing occasionally, until the peas are crisp-tender and the water has evaporated, 2 to 4 minutes. Remove from the heat. Toss with the mint and season with salt and pepper. **SERVES 4**

The combination of mustards in this recipe produces an especially piquant sauce to serve with the pork. Use any leftover pork to make sandwiches the next day.

PORK TENDERLOIN WITH MUSTARD SAUCE

SERVES 6 ■ PREP TIME: 10 MINUTES ■ **TOTAL TIME: 45 MINUTES**

1 tablespoon olive oil
2 pork tenderloins (1 pound each)
Coarse salt and fresh ground pepper
¼ cup whole-grain mustard
2 tablespoons Dijon mustard
2 tablespoons reduced-fat sour cream

1 Heat the olive oil in a large straight-sided skillet over high heat. Season the pork with salt and pepper. Cook until browned on all sides, 5 to 6 minutes.

2 Reduce the heat to medium-low. Cover; cook, turning the pork occasionally, until an instant-read thermometer inserted into the centers registers 150°F, 20 to 25 minutes. Transfer the pork to a plate (reserve the skillet with juices); cover with foil. Let rest 10 minutes.

3 To the skillet, add both mustards, the sour cream, and any accumulated pork juices from the plate; whisk over medium heat until heated through (do not boil). Add water if the sauce is too thick. Slice the pork; serve with the pan sauce.

MIXED GREEN SALAD WITH CITRUS DRESSING

2 tablespoons fresh orange juice
1 tablespoon honey
1 tablespoon minced shallot
2 teaspoons white-wine vinegar
Coarse salt and fresh ground pepper
2 tablespoons extra-virgin olive oil
1 bunch (8 ounces) arugula, stemmed (7 to 8 cups)
4 ounces frisée, torn into bite-size pieces (4 cups)
1 small head (4 ounces) radicchio, torn into bite-size pieces (4 cups)

Combine the juice, honey, shallot, and vinegar in a blender; season with salt and pepper. Purée until smooth. With the motor running, add the oil in a steady stream until emulsified. In a large bowl, toss the arugula, frisée, and radicchio with the dressing; season with more salt and pepper. Serve immediately.
SERVES 4

Mint is a traditional accompaniment for lamb, but in this recipe we use a fresh herb sauce instead of mint jelly.

LAMB CHOPS WITH MINT-PEPPER SAUCE

SERVES 4 ■ PREP TIME: 15 MINUTES ■ TOTAL TIME: 20 MINUTES

- 4 trimmed shoulder lamb chops (each 8 ounces and 1 inch thick)
- 1 tablespoon dried rosemary
  Coarse salt and fresh ground pepper
- 3 tablespoons fresh lemon juice
- 1 tablespoon olive oil
- 2 teaspoons Dijon mustard
- ⅓ cup finely chopped red bell pepper
- ½ cup chopped fresh mint
- 1 scallion, thinly sliced

1 Heat the broiler. Rub both sides of the lamb chops with ¾ teaspoon each dried rosemary and coarse salt and ¼ teaspoon ground pepper. Place the lamb on a broiler pan; broil until the chops are browned, turning once, about 4 minutes per side for medium-rare.

2 Meanwhile, in a small bowl, whisk together the lemon juice, olive oil, and Dijon mustard. Stir in the bell pepper, mint, and scallion. Serve the lamb chops warm, with the sauce spooned over the top.

STEAMED ZUCCHINI WITH SCALLIONS

- Coarse salt
- 3 medium zucchini (about 1½ pounds), cut diagonally into ¼-inch rounds
- 1 tablespoon olive oil
- 2 tablespoons thinly sliced scallions
- Fresh ground pepper

In a large skillet with just enough water to cover the bottom (about ¼ cup). Add ¼ teaspoon salt; bring to a simmer. Add the zucchini. Cook, covered, until tender, 3 to 4 minutes. Drain in a colander, and transfer to a medium bowl. Drizzle the zucchini with the olive oil. Sprinkle with the scallions, and season with salt and pepper; toss to combine.
SERVES 4

The combination of lemon zest, raisins, and pine nuts was inspired by condiments popular in Southern Italian cooking. Try the lemon relish on chicken or pork, or even as a topping for steamed broccoli.

ROASTED SALMON WITH LEMON RELISH

SERVES 4 ■ PREP TIME: 25 MINUTES ■ **TOTAL TIME: 25 MINUTES**

¼ cup pine nuts

¼ cup raisins

Slivered zest and juice of 1 lemon

½ to ¾ cup boiling water

4 skinless salmon fillets (6 ounces each)

Coarse salt and fresh ground pepper

¼ cup chopped fresh parsley

3 tablespoons olive oil

5 ounces baby spinach (about 5 cups, loosely packed)

1 Preheat the oven to 450°F. Spread the pine nuts on a rimmed baking sheet; toast in the oven, tossing occasionally, until lightly golden, 5 to 7 minutes. Remove from the sheet, and reserve.

2 Meanwhile, place the raisins and lemon zest in a small heat-proof bowl; cover with boiling water. Set aside.

3 Place the salmon fillets on the baking sheet used in step 1; season with salt and pepper. Roast until the salmon is opaque throughout, 8 to 10 minutes.

4 Meanwhile, drain and discard the liquid from the raisins and lemon zest. Return the raisins and zest to the bowl; add the lemon juice, pine nuts, parsley, and oil. Season with salt and pepper; stir to combine.

5 Dividing evenly, make a bed of spinach on each of 4 plates. Place a salmon fillet on the spinach; spoon lemon relish over the top.

MAKING LEMON SLIVERS
Use a vegetable peeler to peel the yellow part of the lemon skin into long strips (leaving the white pith behind), before you juice the lemon. Then thinly slice into slivers.

Cod is a lean fish that is available year-round and can be baked, broiled, or poached. Its mild taste pairs well with sharp flavors. Other firm, mild fish, including halibut, sole, or haddock, can be used in place of cod.

COD WITH LEEKS AND TOMATOES

SERVES 4 ■ PREP TIME: 10 MINUTES ■ TOTAL TIME: 35 MINUTES

2 medium leeks, white and light-green parts only, thinly sliced, rinsed well, and patted dry

1 teaspoon freshly grated lemon zest

2 tablespoons fresh lemon juice

1 tablespoon olive oil

3 sprigs thyme or 1 teaspoon dried thyme

Coarse salt and fresh ground pepper

2½ cups cherry tomatoes (about 12 ounces)

4 cod fillets, each 6 to 8 ounces and ¾ to 1 inch thick

1 Preheat the oven to 450°F. In a 9-by-13-inch baking dish, toss together the leeks, lemon zest, lemon juice, oil, thyme, ½ teaspoon salt, and ¼ teaspoon pepper. Cover with foil, and bake until the leeks just begin to soften, 8 to 10 minutes.

2 Remove the baking dish from the oven. Add the tomatoes, and toss to combine. Season both sides of the cod fillets with ½ teaspoon salt and ¼ teaspoon pepper; place on top of the vegetables.

3 Cover the dish and bake until the fish is opaque throughout, 15 to 20 minutes. Serve immediately.

PREPARING THE LEEKS
First cut away and discard the leek's root and dark-green leaves, then thinly slice the white and light-green parts crosswise into rounds. Wash the leek rounds well, as described on page 23. Drain on paper towels.

You can purchase bottled Thai green curry sauce in most supermarkets, but this recipe proves how quick and easy it is to make your own. Refrigerate any leftover sauce, covered, for up to 3 days.

PAN-FRIED SHRIMP WITH GREEN CURRY CASHEW SAUCE

SERVES 4 ■ PREP TIME: 15 MINUTES ■ **TOTAL TIME: 15 MINUTES**

1 slice (¼ inch thick) peeled fresh ginger

¾ cup plus 2 tablespoons roasted unsalted cashews

⅓ cup plain low-fat yogurt

¼ cup packed cilantro leaves

1 tablespoon brown sugar

1 teaspoon curry powder

Coarse salt and fresh ground pepper

1½ pounds peeled and deveined large shrimp

2 tablespoons olive oil

1 In a food processor, pulse the ginger until finely chopped. Add the ¾ cup cashews; process until smooth, 2 to 3 minutes.

2 Add the yogurt, cilantro, sugar, and curry powder; season with salt. Process until incorporated, 1 to 2 minutes, scraping down the sides as needed. Transfer to a serving bowl; sprinkle with the remaining cashews.

3 Season the shrimp with salt and pepper. Heat 1 tablespoon of the oil in a large nonstick skillet over medium-high heat. Add half the shrimp; cook until opaque throughout, 2 to 3 minutes. Repeat with the remaining tablespoon oil and remaining shrimp. Serve the shrimp with the sauce.

SESAME CARROT SALAD

1 pound (5 to 6 medium) carrots, peeled and coarsely grated

2 tablespoons sesame seeds

1 to 2 tablespoons rice vinegar

1 tablespoon toasted sesame oil

1 piece (1 inch) fresh ginger, peeled and finely chopped (about 2 tablespoons)

Coarse salt and fresh ground pepper

In a large bowl, combine the carrots, sesame seeds, vinegar, oil, and ginger. Season with salt and pepper; toss to combine. **SERVES 4**

PREP TIME **30** MINUTES

The combination of anchovy paste and soy sauce is a good substitution for Asian fish sauce, which is used to flavor many Thai dishes. If you have fish sauce on hand, use 2 tablespoons and omit the anchovy paste and soy sauce.

SHRIMP PAD THAI

SERVES 6 ■ PREP TIME: 30 MINUTES ■ TOTAL TIME: 45 MINUTES

8 ounces rice-stick noodles

¼ cup tomato-based chile sauce

¼ cup fresh lime juice

3 tablespoons soy sauce

2 tablespoons light brown sugar

1 tablespoon anchovy paste

4 tablespoons vegetable oil

4 garlic cloves, minced

1 pound peeled and deveined medium shrimp

3 cups bean sprouts, plus more for garnish

8 scallions, trimmed, halved lengthwise, and cut crosswise into 2-inch pieces

1 large egg, lightly beaten

Assorted garnishes, optional:

⅓ cup chopped dry-roasted peanuts

Pinch of red pepper flakes

1 cup bean sprouts

¼ cup fresh cilantro

Lime wedges

1 Bring a large pot of water to a boil; remove from the heat. Stir in the noodles; let soak until softened (but still undercooked), 3 minutes. Drain; rinse under cold water until cool.

2 In a small bowl, whisk together the chile sauce, lime juice, soy sauce, brown sugar, and anchovy paste. In a large nonstick skillet, heat 2 table-spoons of the oil over medium-high heat. Add the garlic, and cook until fragrant, about 30 seconds. Add the shrimp; cook, tossing often, until just opaque throughout, about 3 min-utes. Transfer the shrimp to a plate.

3 Return the skillet to medium-high heat. Add the remaining 2 tablespoons oil along with the noodles and chile sauce mixture; cook, tossing, until com-bined, about 1 minute. Add the bean sprouts, scallions, and shrimp. Pour in the egg; toss until the noodles are coated and cooked through, about 2 minutes. Serve topped with garnishes, if desired.

PREPARING RICE NOODLES
Rice noodles are very delicate; for best results, have the other ingredients cut and measured before you begin, and make sure to undercook the noodles in the first step.

Niçoise salads are usually made with tuna, but we substituted fresh salmon in this version. You can, of course, make the salad with a couple of cans of tuna; look for Italian oil-packed tuna, which has the best flavor.

SALMON NIÇOISE SALAD

SERVES 4 ■ PREP TIME: 30 MINUTES ■ TOTAL TIME: 45 MINUTES

Coarse salt and
fresh ground pepper

12 ounces (4 to 5) red new potatoes

8 ounces green beans, trimmed

2 skinless salmon fillets
(about 8 ounces each)

2 heads Boston lettuce

4 plum tomatoes

3 large eggs, hard-cooked
(see page 348)

1 medium red onion

1 jar or tin (2.8 ounces) anchovy
fillets, drained (optional)

¼ cup kalamata (or black) olives
Dijon Vinaigrette (recipe below)

DIJON VINAIGRETTE

2 tablespoons fresh lemon juice

1 tablespoon Dijon mustard
Coarse salt and
fresh ground pepper

¼ cup olive oil

1 In a medium bowl, whisk the juice, mustard, ½ teaspoon salt, and a pinch of pepper until combined.

2 Whisking constantly, add the olive oil in a steady stream; whisk until thickened and creamy. (Alternatively, shake all ingredients in a small jar.)

1 In a 5-quart pot, bring ½ inch water to a boil; add salt and the potatoes. Cover; cook, turning occasionally, until tender, 14 to 16 minutes.

2 With a slotted spoon, transfer the potatoes to a bowl. Set aside to cool. Add the green beans to the pot of boiling water. Cover; cook, turning occasionally, until tender, 4 to 6 minutes. Remove with a slotted spoon. Rinse under cool water, and set aside.

3 Fill a deep skillet with ¼ inch water. Season the salmon on both sides with salt and pepper; place in the skillet. Bring the water to a gentle simmer; cover, and cook until the salmon is opaque throughout, 10 to 12 minutes. Transfer to a plate; flake with a fork, and let cool.

4 While the salmon is cooking, tear lettuce into pieces, quarter the potatoes and tomatoes, peel and quarter the eggs (use a wet paring knife to make neat cuts), and thinly slice the onion.

5 On a large platter (or 4 serving plates), arrange the lettuce, salmon, green beans, potatoes, eggs, tomatoes, onion, anchovies (if using), and olives. Serve with the vinaigrette.

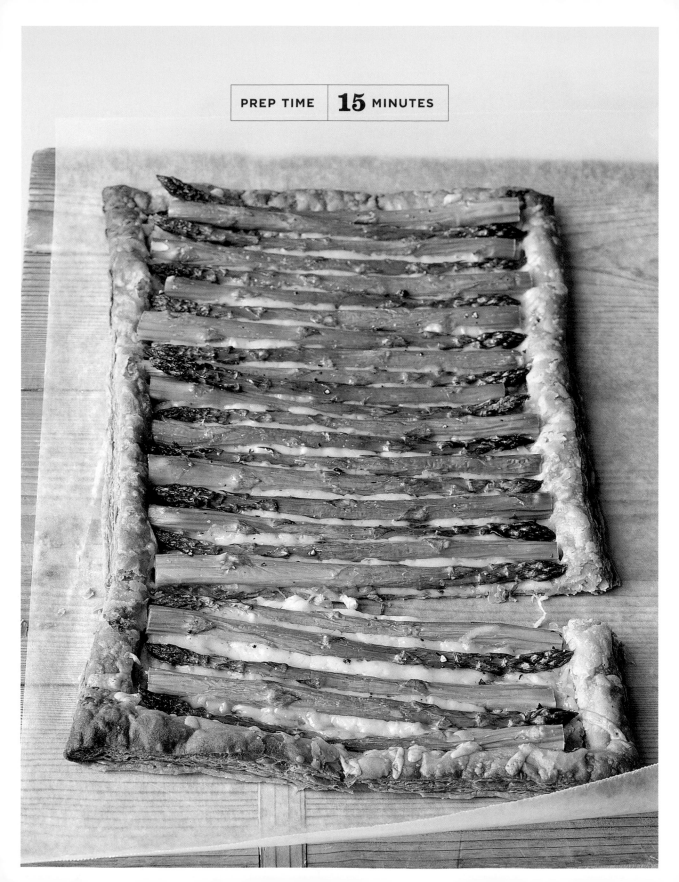

Although it takes just minutes to put together, this savory tart makes an impressive main course. A simple green salad completes the meal. The tart is also a lovely addition to a buffet or a potluck.

ASPARAGUS GRUYÈRE TART

SERVES 4 ■ PREP TIME: 15 MINUTES ■ **TOTAL TIME: 45 MINUTES**

Flour, for work surface

1 sheet frozen puff pastry (from a 17.3-ounce package), thawed according to package instructions

5½ ounces Gruyère cheese, shredded (2 cups)

1½ pounds medium or thick asparagus

1 tablespoon olive oil

Coarse salt and fresh ground pepper

1 Preheat the oven to 400°F. On a lightly floured surface, roll the puff pastry into a 16-by-10-inch rectangle. Trim uneven edges. Place the pastry on a baking sheet. With a sharp knife, lightly score the dough 1 inch in from the edges to mark a rectangle. Using a fork, pierce the dough inside the markings at half-inch intervals. Bake until golden, about 15 minutes.

2 Remove the pastry shell from the oven, and sprinkle with the cheese. Trim the bottoms of the asparagus spears to fit crosswise inside the tart shell; arrange in a single layer over the cheese, alternating ends and tips. Brush with the oil, and season with salt and pepper. Bake until the spears are tender, 20 to 25 minutes.

SCORING THE DOUGH
Use a sharp knife to ensure that the edges rise evenly; pricking the center of the pastry with a fork keeps it from puffing up too high as it bakes.

Rich and creamy, risotto is Italian-style comfort food. If you like, replace the wine with an equal amount of broth. Arborio rice makes the creamiest risotto, but you can substitute medium- or long-grain white rice.

SPRING RISOTTO WITH PEAS AND ZUCCHINI

SERVES 6 ■ PREP TIME: 1 HOUR ■ **TOTAL TIME: 1 HOUR**

2 cans (14.5 ounces each) reduced-sodium chicken broth

3 tablespoons butter

1 to 2 large zucchini (1 pound), cut into ½-inch cubes

Coarse salt and fresh ground pepper

½ cup finely chopped onion

1½ cups Arborio rice

½ cup dry white wine

1 cup frozen peas, thawed

½ cup grated Parmesan cheese, plus more for garnish

1 Heat the broth and 2½ cups water in a saucepan over low heat; keep warm. Meanwhile, melt 2 tablespoons of the butter in a 3-quart saucepan over medium heat. Add the zucchini; season with salt and pepper. Cook, stirring often, until the zucchini is golden, 8 to 10 minutes. With a slotted spoon, transfer the zucchini to a plate.

2 Reduce the heat to medium-low. Add the onion; cook until soft, 5 minutes. Season with 1 teaspoon salt and ¼ teaspoon pepper. Raise the heat to medium. Add the rice; cook, stirring, until translucent around the edges, about 3 minutes. Add the wine; cook until absorbed, about 2 minutes.

3 Cook the rice, adding 1 cup hot broth at a time (stir until almost all the liquid is absorbed before adding more), until tender, 25 to 30 minutes total.

4 Add the zucchini and peas; cook until the peas are bright green, 2 minutes. Remove from the heat. Stir in the remaining tablespoon butter and the Parmesan. Serve, topped with more cheese.

Take a break from ordinary tomato sauce with this crowd-pleasing pasta dish. Leaf-Lettuce Salad with Parmesan Crisps (page 27) makes a perfect starter.

SPAGHETTI WITH THREE-TOMATO SAUCE

SERVES 4 ■ PREP TIME: 10 MINUTES ■ **TOTAL TIME: 35 MINUTES**

Coarse salt and
fresh ground pepper
1 pound spaghetti
½ cup oil-packed sun-dried tomatoes, chopped, oil reserved
4 garlic cloves, minced
¼ to ½ teaspoon red pepper flakes
1 can (28 ounces) whole peeled tomatoes
1 pound cherry tomatoes, halved

1 In a large pot of boiling salted water, cook the spaghetti until al dente according to the package directions. Drain, reserving 1 cup of the pasta water; return the pasta to the pot.

2 Meanwhile, heat 2 tablespoons sun-dried tomato oil in a large saucepan over medium heat. Add the garlic and red pepper flakes; cook until fragrant, 30 seconds. Add the canned tomatoes (with juice) and sun-dried tomatoes. Simmer gently, stirring occasionally and breaking up the canned tomatoes, until thick, about 15 minutes.

3 Add the cherry tomatoes; simmer until soft, about 10 minutes.

4 Add to the pasta. Season with salt and pepper. Toss, adding pasta water as desired. Serve immediately.

This classic Italian combination is made light and bright with turkey sausage and yellow bell peppers. Arugula gives the dish a peppery taste.

LINGUINE WITH SAUSAGE AND PEPPERS

SERVES 6 ■ PREP TIME: 15 MINUTES ■ **TOTAL TIME: 30 MINUTES**

Coarse salt and
fresh ground pepper
1 pound linguine
1 pound turkey sausage,
casings removed
6 garlic cloves, thinly sliced
4 yellow or red bell peppers, ribs
and seeds removed, thinly sliced
4 tablespoons butter
4 cups arugula, torn

1 In a large pot of boiling salted water, cook the linguine until al dente according to the package directions. Drain, reserving 1½ cups of the pasta water; return the pasta to the pot.

2 Meanwhile, cook the sausage and 2 tablespoons water in a large covered nonstick skillet over medium until the fat renders, about 5 minutes. Uncover; raise the heat to medium-high. Brown the sausage, breaking it up with a spoon, about 7 minutes.

3 Add the garlic, bell peppers, and ¼ cup of the reserved pasta water; cook until the peppers soften, about 6 minutes. Add ¾ cup of the pasta water and the butter; swirl to combine.

4 Transfer to the pot. Add the arugula; season with coarse salt and ground pepper. Toss; add more pasta water as desired. Serve immediately.

In this one-pot dish the spinach cooks alongside the pasta. Spoon ricotta and pine nuts onto each serving, and let your guests mix them into the pasta themselves.

SPINACH PENNE WITH RICOTTA AND PINE NUTS

SERVES 6 ■ PREP TIME: 10 MINUTES ■ **TOTAL TIME: 20 MINUTES**

⅓ cup pine nuts
1 pound spinach penne
1½ pounds baby spinach, well washed
2 tablespoons olive oil
   Coarse salt and fresh ground pepper
1 cup part-skim ricotta cheese
¼ cup grated Parmesan cheese

1 Preheat the oven to 350°F. Spread the pine nuts on a rimmed baking sheet; toast in the oven, tossing occasionally, until golden, 6 to 8 minutes; set aside.

2 Meanwhile, in a large pot of boiling salted water, cook the spinach penne until al dente according to package directions, adding the fresh spinach during the last 2 minutes of cooking. Drain; return the pasta and spinach to the pot.

3 Add the olive oil; season generously with salt and pepper. Toss well.

4 Serve immediately, topped with the ricotta, pine nuts, and Parmesan.

Adding a bit of the pasta cooking water thins the goat cheese- and mustard-based sauce and helps it adhere to the fettuccine.

CREAMY FETTUCCINE WITH ASPARAGUS

SERVES 4 ■ PREP TIME: 15 MINUTES ■ **TOTAL TIME: 30 MINUTES**

¼ cup pine nuts
 Coarse salt and
 fresh ground pepper
¾ pound fettuccine
 (or other thick-stranded pasta)
2 bunches asparagus, trimmed,
 halved lengthwise, and
 cut crosswise into thirds
4 ounces creamy goat cheese,
 broken into pieces
2 tablespoons grainy mustard
2 tablespoons snipped
 fresh dill leaves

1 In a small skillet over medium heat, toast the pine nuts, stirring often, until golden, 2 to 3 minutes.

2 In a large pot of boiling salted water, cook the fettuccine until al dente, according to the package instructions, adding the asparagus during the last 5 minutes of cooking. Reserve 1 cup of the pasta water; drain.

3 Return pasta, asparagus, and reserved pasta water to the pot. Toss with the goat cheese, mustard, dill, and toasted pine nuts. Season with salt and pepper. Serve immediately.

This pasta features a few flavors of the season—mint and peas—along with lemon and ever-popular salmon. It's just the thing to hit the spot on a crisp spring evening.

FARFALLE WITH SALMON, MINT, AND PEAS

SERVES 6 ■ PREP TIME: 10 MINUTES ■ **TOTAL TIME: 30 MINUTES**

Coarse salt and
fresh ground pepper
1 pound farfalle
1½ pounds skinless salmon fillet
2 lemons, zested and juiced
1 package (10 ounces) frozen peas
2 tablespoons butter
¼ cup chopped fresh mint,
plus more for serving

1 In a large pot of boiling salted water, cook the farfalle until al dente according to the package directions. Drain, reserving 1 cup of the pasta water; return the pasta to the pot.

2 Meanwhile, season the salmon with coarse salt and ground pepper; place in a large skillet. Add ¼ cup water and the lemon zest and juice. Bring to a simmer over medium heat. Cover; steam for 10 minutes.

3 Add the frozen peas; steam, covered, until the peas are tender and the salmon is opaque, 6 to 8 minutes.

4 Transfer to the pot with the pasta. Add the butter and mint. Season with salt and pepper. Toss, gently flaking the fish and adding reserved pasta water as desired. Serve immediately, sprinkled with more mint.

CUCUMBER-RADISH SLAW

2 English cucumbers
4 to 6 radishes
  Coarse salt and fresh ground pepper
2 tablespoons minced red onion
3 tablespoons cider vinegar
2 teaspoons olive oil
1 teaspoon sugar

1 Peel the cucumbers. Halve lengthwise; scrape out any seeds with a teaspoon. Slice the cucumbers very thin on the diagonal.

2 Thinly slice enough radishes to equal 1 cup. In a large colander, toss the vegetables with ½ teaspoon salt. Top the mixture with a plate that fits inside the colander; weight with a heavy object. Drain in the sink for 20 minutes; squeeze the vegetables in paper towels to dry.

3 Transfer to a bowl; toss with the onion, vinegar, olive oil, and sugar; season with salt and pepper. Serve immediately. SERVES 4

GINGERED SUGAR SNAPS

1 tablespoon vegetable oil
1 pound sugar snaps, strings removed
1 piece (1 inch) peeled fresh ginger, finely chopped (about 1 tablespoon)
  Coarse salt and fresh ground pepper

1 In a 12-inch skillet, heat the oil over medium high. Add the sugar snaps and ginger. Cook, stirring occasionally, until the snaps begin to brown, about 5 minutes.

2 Add ¼ cup water; reduce the heat to medium. Cook, stirring and scraping up the ginger from the bottom of the skillet with a wooden spoon, until the snaps are crisp-tender, about 2 minutes. Season with salt and pepper. SERVES 4

PARMESAN STEAK FRIES

3 large egg whites
  Coarse salt and fresh ground pepper
3 baking potatoes
  (8 to 10 ounces each)
1¼ cups grated Parmesan cheese

1 Preheat the oven to 425°F. In a wide, shallow bowl, whisk the egg whites with 1 teaspoon salt until frothy. Cut each potato into 6 long spears; add to the egg whites, and turn to coat.

2 One at a time, lift the spears out of the egg whites, shaking off excess; working over a plate, sprinkle with the Parmesan cheese until coated (do not shake off excess). Place on a parchment-lined baking sheet.

3 Bake, without turning, until the potatoes are fork-tender and golden brown, about 30 minutes. Season with salt and pepper. SERVES 4

CHERRY TOMATO CRISP

2 slices white sandwich bread
¼ cup grated Parmesan cheese
2 tablespoons fresh parsley leaves
1 tablespoon olive oil
1 garlic clove, chopped
  Coarse salt and fresh ground pepper
1½ pounds cherry tomatoes
  (about 5 cups)

1 Preheat the oven to 400°F. In a food processor, combine the bread, Parmesan cheese, parsley, olive oil, and garlic; season with salt and pepper. Pulse until bread is very coarsely chopped, 4 to 6 times.

2 In an 8-inch square baking dish, arrange the cherry tomatoes in a single layer; sprinkle with the crumb mixture. Bake until the crust is browned and the tomatoes are tender, 20 to 25 minutes. SERVES 4

SPINACH WITH ORZO AND FETA

Coarse salt and fresh ground pepper
½ pound orzo
1 pound spinach, trimmed and chopped
½ cup chopped fresh mint
½ cup crumbled feta cheese
1 to 2 tablespoons fresh lemon juice
1 tablespoon olive oil

1 In a large pot of boiling salted water, cook the orzo according to the package instructions. Stir in the spinach until wilted. Drain.

2 In a large bowl, toss the hot spinach and orzo with the remaining ingredients. Season with salt and pepper. **SERVES 4**

GLAZED CARROTS

9 carrots (1½ pounds), quartered and cut into 2-inch lengths
1 tablespoon sugar
2 tablespoons butter
½ teaspoon coarse salt
Fresh ground pepper

1 In a skillet, bring the carrots, sugar, butter, salt, and ½ cup water to a boil. Reduce heat; simmer, partly covered, 6 minutes.

2 Cook uncovered, over high heat, tossing often until tender, 3 to 4 minutes. Season with pepper. **SERVES 4**

WARM WHITE BEAN SALAD

1 tablespoon olive oil
½ small red onion, diced
2 medium carrots, halved lengthwise and thinly sliced
1 medium red bell pepper, ribs and seeds removed, diced
1 garlic clove, slivered
1 can (19 ounces) cannellini beans, drained and rinsed
1 teaspoon grated lemon zest
Coarse salt and fresh ground pepper
2 teaspoons fresh lemon juice

In a small saucepan, heat the oil over medium heat. Add the onion and carrots; cook, stirring frequently, until the onion is lightly browned, about 5 minutes. Add bell pepper and garlic; cook, stirring, until pepper is crisp-tender, about 3 minutes. Stir in beans, lemon zest, and 1 cup water, and season with salt and pepper; bring to a boil. Reduce to a simmer; cover, and cook until beans have absorbed most of the liquid, about 10 minutes. Stir in the lemon juice; season again with salt and pepper. **SERVES 4**

ROASTED ASPARAGUS WITH PARMESAN

2 bunches (1½ pounds) asparagus
1 tablespoon olive oil
Coarse salt and fresh ground pepper
¼ cup finely grated Parmesan cheese

1 Preheat the oven to 450°F. Trim the tough ends from the asparagus.

2 On a rimmed baking sheet, toss the asparagus with the olive oil; season with salt and pepper. Spread in an even layer. Sprinkle with the Parmesan cheese.

3 Roast until the asparagus is tender and the cheese is melted, 10 to 15 minutes. Serve immediately. **SERVES 4**

These treats aren't fancy; they're just plain good and full of memories. You can prepare the strawberries up to a day ahead, but wait until just before serving the dessert to assemble it.

STRAWBERRY SHORTCAKES

SERVES 8 ■ PREP TIME: 30 MINUTES ■ **TOTAL TIME: 1 HOUR**

2½ cups all-purpose flour (spooned and leveled), plus more for dusting

⅓ cup (about ⅔ stick) cold unsalted butter, cut into small pieces

⅓ cup plus 1 tablespoon sugar

2½ teaspoons baking powder

1 teaspoon salt

1 cup milk

Sweetened Strawberries (recipe below)

Whipped Cream (page 363)

1 Preheat the oven to 425°F. In a food processor, combine the flour, butter, ⅓ cup sugar, baking powder, and salt; process until the mixture resembles coarse meal. Add the milk; pulse just until moistened, 4 or 5 times. Do not overprocess.

2 Turn out the dough onto a lightly floured surface; with floured hands, gently pat the dough into a 4-by-8-inch rectangle.

3 Dust a large knife with flour; cut the dough into 8 squares. Transfer to a baking sheet; sprinkle with the remaining tablespoon sugar. Bake until golden, 25 to 30 minutes; cool on the baking sheet. To serve, split the biscuits with a serrated knife; layer with the berries and whipped cream.

SWEETENED STRAWBERRIES

1½ pounds (about 6 cups) fresh strawberries

¼ cup sugar

Hull and quarter the strawberries; toss in a medium bowl with the sugar. Let stand until syrupy, tossing occasionally, at least 20 minutes (and up to 1 day, covered and refrigerated).

Rhubarb is a vegetable, although it is typically used in jams and desserts; its tart flavor makes it the perfect companion for fresh strawberries, or in this case, strawberry ice cream.

RHUBARB CRISP

SERVES 12 ■ PREP TIME: 15 MINUTES ■ **TOTAL TIME: 50 MINUTES**

2 pounds rhubarb

1½ cups sugar

¾ cup flour

½ cup (1 stick) unsalted butter, chilled, cut into pieces

1 cup rolled oats

½ teaspoon ground cinnamon
Strawberry ice cream, for serving (optional)

1 Preheat the oven to 400°F. Slice the rhubarb stalks on the diagonal into uniform ¾-inch-thick pieces. Place in a 9-by-13-inch baking dish; toss with 1 cup of the sugar and ¼ cup of the flour.

2 In a food processor, pulse the remaining ½ cup flour with the butter until the clumps are pea-size. Add the remaining ½ cup sugar, the rolled oats, and cinnamon; pulse just to combine. Sprinkle over the rhubarb.

3 Bake until the rhubarb is tender and the topping is golden, 35 minutes. Serve warm with ice cream, if desired.

Baking the desserts in a hot-water bath keeps them creamy and custardy beneath their golden, cakey tops. Lining the roasting pan with a dish towel helps the water circulate under the cups for even cooking.

LEMON CUSTARD CAKES

SERVES 6 ■ PREP TIME: 20 MINUTES ■ **TOTAL TIME: 45 MINUTES**

Unsalted butter, at room temperature, for custard cups

3 large eggs, separated

½ cup granulated sugar

2 tablespoons all-purpose flour

2 to 3 teaspoons grated lemon zest (from 1 lemon)

¼ cup fresh lemon juice

1 cup milk

¼ teaspoon salt

Confectioners' sugar, for dusting

1 Preheat the oven to 350°F. Set a kettle of water to boil. Butter six 6-ounce custard cups, and place them in a roasting pan or baking dish lined with a kitchen towel.

2 In a large bowl, whisk together the egg yolks and granulated sugar until the mixture is light; whisk in the flour. Gradually whisk in the lemon zest and juice, then whisk in the milk.

3 With an electric mixer, beat the egg whites and salt until soft peaks form. Add to the lemon mixture; gently fold in with a whisk (the batter will be thin).

4 Divide the batter among the prepared cups. Place the pan in the oven, and fill with boiling water to reach halfway up the sides of the cups. Bake until the puddings are puffed and lightly browned, 20 to 25 minutes. Serve warm or at room temperature, dusted with confectioners' sugar.

NOTE
If you do not have individual custard cups, bake the batter in an 8-inch square baking dish (or other shallow 2-quart baking dish) for 30 to 35 minutes.

PREP TIME | **20** MINUTES

Here's a foolproof recipe that involves nothing more than assembling a few store-bought ingredients with a five-minute chocolate sauce. Make it once and it'll soon become a stand-by whenever you want a little something sweet.

CHOCOLATE-SAUCE GRASSHOPPER SUNDAES

SERVES 4
PREP TIME: 5 MINUTES
TOTAL TIME: 5 MINUTES

12 store-bought chocolate wafer cookies

1 pint mint chocolate-chip ice cream

½ cup Chocolate Sauce (page 362), chilled for about 30 minutes, or store-bought chocolate sauce

Fresh mint, for garnish

1 Divide the cookies and ice cream among 4 serving dishes.

2 Dividing evenly, drizzle with the chocolate sauce; garnish with mint. Serve immediately.

When iced, these carrot-filled cupcakes make heavenly desserts or snacks. Unfrosted, they are perfect for breakfast on the run or a lunch-box treat. Use the large holes of a box grater, or the shredding disk of a food processor, to shred the carrots.

CARROT CUPCAKES

MAKES 12 ■ PREP TIME: 25 MINUTES ■ TOTAL TIME: 50 MINUTES

1¼ cups shredded coconut

1 cup sugar

⅓ cup vegetable oil, plus more for pan, if needed

2 tablespoons fresh orange juice

½ teaspoon vanilla extract

2 large eggs

1 teaspoon baking powder

½ teaspoon baking soda

½ teaspoon ground allspice

½ teaspoon salt

¾ cup plus 2 tablespoons flour

1½ cups shredded carrots

½ cup chopped walnuts

Cream Cheese Icing (recipe below)

1 Preheat the oven to 350°F. Spread 1 cup of the shredded coconut out on a baking sheet, and toast in the oven until golden brown, about 5 minutes. Transfer the coconut to a small bowl and set aside to cool.

2 In a bowl, combine the sugar, ⅓ cup oil, orange juice, vanilla, and eggs. Stir in the baking powder, baking soda, allspice, and salt. Add the flour; mix. Stir in the shredded carrots, the walnuts, and the remaining ¼ cup shredded coconut.

3 Oil a standard muffin tin or line with paper muffin liners; distribute the batter evenly.

4 Bake until a toothpick inserted in the centers comes out clean, about 25 minutes. Let the cupcakes cool before frosting with cream cheese icing. Garnish with reserved toasted shredded coconut.

CREAM CHEESE ICING

8 ounces cream cheese, at room temperature

¾ cup confectioners' sugar

¼ teaspoon vanilla extract

In a mixing bowl, whisk the cream cheese, sugar, and vanilla together until smooth. Use immediately, or store in the refrigerator in an airtight container for up to 5 days.

PREP TIME | **25** MINUTES

SUMMER

AS SPRING GIVES WAY TO SUMMER, the dinner hour often stretches later into the evening. Yet longer daylight hours don't always translate into more time to make the main meal. In fact, with laid-back schedules and outdoor activities, it can be just as difficult to get dinner on the table quickly as it is throughout the rest of the year.

That's why summertime meals rely on fast methods like grilling, along with flavor enhancers like marinades, rubs, and barbecue sauces. These usually take only minutes to make, yet they coax loads of flavor from meats, chicken, vegetables, and fish. This chapter also includes both familiar and unexpected variations on that backyard classic—the burger.

Naturally, there are also dozens of ideas for summer vegetables, including fresh corn grilled in the husk, or cut from the cob and used as the base for a creamy soup, savory fritters, or a picnic-worthy side dish. Salads and desserts take similar advantage of seasonal produce, and as the ultimate time-saver, scoops of store-bought ice cream are rolled in a variety of crunchy, delicious toppings, a perfectly carefree way to cool off after an extra-long day in the sun.

Capture the sweetness of fresh corn in this three-ingredient soup. Freeze portions for up to six months, then heat them straight from the freezer.

CREAMY CORN SOUP

SERVES 8 ■ PREP TIME: 20 MINUTES ■ **TOTAL TIME: 25 MINUTES**

16 ears yellow corn
4 tablespoons butter, cut into small pieces
Coarse salt

Suggested garnishes:
Tortilla chips
Lime wedges
Sliced scallions

1 Remove the husks and silks from the corn. Holding the ears in a large bowl, slice off the kernels (to yield about 10 cups). In two batches, purée the kernels and accumulated juices with a total of 2 cups water until chunky.

2 In a large saucepan over medium-high heat, cook the puréed corn, butter, 4 cups water, and 1 tablespoon coarse salt until the butter is melted and the soup is heated through, 5 minutes.

3 Serve hot with suggested garnishes, as desired. Or let cool, then freeze in individual servings; reheat over medium-low (or in the microwave).

A cup of this soup is delicious, served hot or cold. Try packing it in a thermos for a light picnic lunch. To chill quickly, place the soup in a bowl and set that bowl into an ice-water bath. Stir frequently until cool.

CURRIED ZUCCHINI SOUP

SERVES 4 ■ PREP TIME: 25 MINUTES ■ TOTAL TIME: 40 MINUTES

1 tablespoon olive oil
1 medium onion, chopped
  Coarse salt
2 garlic cloves, minced
2 teaspoons curry powder
1½ pounds zucchini (about
  3 medium), sliced 1 inch thick
1 baking potato, peeled
  and cut into 1-inch chunks
⅓ cup sliced almonds, toasted,
  for garnish

1 Heat the oil in a large saucepan over medium heat. Add the onion and 1 tablespoon salt; cook, stirring occasionally, until the onion is soft, 4 to 5 minutes. Add the garlic and curry powder; cook, stirring constantly, until fragrant, about 1 minute.

2 Add the zucchini, potato, and 4 cups water. Bring to a boil; reduce the heat, and simmer until the vegetables are tender, 10 to 15 minutes.

3 In batches, purée the soup in a blender (do not fill more than halfway) until smooth; serve immediately, or let cool, and refrigerate in an airtight container until chilled. Garnish with the toasted almonds.

Gazpacho is traditionally made by adding olive oil to vegetable purée; in this light version, we left out the oil and used only a small amount to cook the shrimp.

SHRIMP GAZPACHO

SERVES 4 ■ PREP TIME: 25 MINUTES ■ TOTAL TIME: 35 MINUTES

1 tablespoon olive oil

1 pound medium shrimp, peeled and deveined, tails removed (see note below)

Coarse salt and fresh ground pepper

6 plum tomatoes, chopped (about 3 cups)

½ small red onion, chopped

2 garlic cloves, chopped

½ cucumber, peeled and chopped

½ cup finely chopped jarred roasted bell peppers (we used both red and yellow peppers)

1½ cups tomato juice

2 tablespoons red-wine vinegar

1 In a large nonstick skillet, heat the oil over high heat, swirling to coat the bottom of the pan. Season the shrimp with salt and pepper. Add half the shrimp; cook until browned on both sides and opaque in the center, 3 to 4 minutes. Transfer to a plate; repeat with the remaining shrimp (reduce the heat if browning too quickly).

2 In a food processor, combine the tomatoes, onion, garlic, cucumber, and half the roasted peppers; process until combined. Add the tomato juice and vinegar; process until smooth. Season with salt and pepper.

3 To serve, divide the tomato mixture among the bowls; top with the shrimp and the remaining roasted peppers.

DEVEINING SHRIMP
Peel the shrimp and remove the tail. Make a shallow incision down the middle of the back with a sharp knife; scrape (or pull) out the dark vein.

Using a variety of colorful tomatoes makes a stunning presentation. The dressing is simple—since tomatoes are so flavorful in the summer, they don't need much accompaniment.

MIXED TOMATO SALAD

SERVES 4
PREP TIME: 15 MINUTES
TOTAL TIME: 15 MINUTES

- 2 pounds mixed tomatoes, such as red or yellow beefsteak, cherry, grape, and pear
- 3 tablespoons red-wine vinegar
- 3 tablespoons extra-virgin olive oil
  Coarse salt and fresh ground pepper
- 1 bunch arugula (6 to 8 ounces), washed well and dried

1 Core the beefsteak tomatoes; cut each into 8 wedges. Halve the grape and cherry tomatoes; leave the pear tomatoes whole.

2 Make the dressing: In a small bowl, whisk together the vinegar and oil; season with salt and pepper. In a large bowl, toss the arugula with half the dressing. Divide the arugula and tomatoes evenly among 4 serving plates, or arrange on a platter; drizzle the tomatoes with the remaining dressing. Serve immediately.

In Italy, prosciutto and melon are combined in a traditional first course. Here, cool, silky bocconcini and torn mint leaves are added to make a refreshing salad—just the thing to begin a meal on a warm summer night.

CANTALOUPE AND BOCCONCINI SALAD WITH MINT

SERVES 4 ■ PREP TIME: 15 MINUTES ■ TOTAL TIME: 15 MINUTES

1 ripe cantaloupe

8 ounces bocconcini (small fresh mozzarella balls), or fresh mozzarella cut into 1-inch cubes (about 2 cups)

2 to 3 thin slices ham or prosciutto, cut into strips

1 tablespoon fresh lemon juice
  Coarse salt and
  fresh ground pepper

¼ cup torn mint leaves

1 Scoop the cantaloupe into 1-inch balls with a melon baller; you should have about 3 cups. In a large bowl, combine the cantaloupe balls, bocconcini, ham, and lemon juice; season with salt and pepper.

2 Toss the salad with the mint, and serve immediately.

When you find yourself with day-old bread, make this Tuscan salad, known as panzanella. Coarse-textured, good-quality bread works best. Feel free to improvise by adding olives, anchovies, or canned tuna.

TOMATO AND GRILLED BREAD SALAD

SERVES 4 ■ PREP TIME: 25 MINUTES ■ TOTAL TIME: 25 MINUTES

½ pound country bread, cut into ¾-inch-thick slices

¼ cup plus 2 tablespoons olive oil

3 large beefsteak tomatoes, cut into ¾-inch dice (about 4 cups)

1 cucumber, peeled and cut into ¾-inch dice (about 2 cups)

¼ cup loosely packed fresh basil, torn into bite-size pieces

1 tablespoon red-wine vinegar
Coarse salt and fresh ground pepper

1 Heat a grill to medium. Brush the bread slices on both sides with the 2 tablespoons oil. Grill until lightly charred on both sides, 3 to 4 minutes. Let the bread cool slightly, then cut into large cubes.

2 In a large bowl, toss the bread cubes with the diced tomatoes, cucumber, and basil. Drizzle with the vinegar and the remaining ¼ cup oil, and season with salt and pepper. Toss to combine, and serve.

This summer salad has it all—crunchy, peppery greens; soft, smooth cheese; and sweet, smoky, slightly caramelized peaches hot off the grill.

WATERCRESS, ENDIVE, AND GRILLED PEACH SALAD

SERVES 4 ■ PREP TIME: 20 MINUTES ■ **TOTAL TIME: 20 MINUTES**

2 peaches, halved and pitted

1 tablespoon melted unsalted butter

2 tablespoons fresh lemon juice

2 tablespoons olive oil

Coarse salt and fresh ground pepper

2 Belgian endives, trimmed and cut crosswise into 1-inch pieces

2 bunches stemmed watercress (about 8 cups)

6 ounces bocconcini (small fresh mozzarella balls), halved, or sliced fresh mozzarella

1 Heat a grill to medium-low. Brush both sides of the peaches with the melted butter.

2 Place the peaches on the grill; cover the grill, and cook until the peaches are charred and softened, 4 to 5 minutes per side. Quarter each half, and set aside.

3 In a large bowl, whisk the lemon juice and olive oil; season with salt and pepper.

4 Add the endives, watercress, and bocconcini. Toss to coat. Divide among 4 plates; arrange the peaches next to the salad.

The barbecue sauce in this recipe is so easy and quick to put together, you may never rely on store-bought sauce again. And what's more, you probably already have all of the necessary ingredients in your kitchen.

BARBECUED CHICKEN

SERVES 4 ■ PREP TIME: 20 MINUTES ■ TOTAL TIME: 30 MINUTES

 1 teaspoon hot sauce
 ⅓ cup cider vinegar
 ½ cup light brown sugar
 ¼ cup molasses
 3 tablespoons Dijon mustard
 3 garlic cloves, minced
 ½ cup ketchup
 1 cut-up chicken (3 pounds)
 1 tablespoon vegetable oil, plus more for grates
   Coarse salt and fresh ground pepper

1 Heat a grill to medium. Simmer the hot sauce, vinegar, brown sugar, molasses, mustard, garlic, and ketchup in a small saucepan over medium heat until reduced to about 1¼ cups, 5 to 7 minutes.

2 In a large bowl, toss the chicken with the vegetable oil; season well with salt and pepper.

3 Lightly oil the grates; place the chicken on the grill. Cover the grill; cook, turning frequently, until the chicken registers 165°F (160°F for the breast) on an instant-read thermometer, 10 to 15 minutes. Uncover the grill; continue cooking, basting frequently with the sauce, until the chicken is glazed thoroughly, 3 to 4 minutes more. Serve with the remaining sauce.

CORN AND RADISH SALAD

   Coarse salt
 4 ears corn
 6 radishes, trimmed, halved, and thinly sliced
 1 jalapeño chile, finely chopped (ribs and seeds removed for less heat, if desired)
 2 tablespoons fresh lime juice
 1 tablespoon olive oil

In a large pot of boiling salted water, cook the corn until fragrant and tender, 8 to 12 minutes. Remove the ears, and hold under cold water until completely cool. Working in a large bowl, slice the kernels from the cobs (to yield about 2 cups). Toss with the radishes, jalapeño, lime juice, and olive oil. Season generously with salt. Serve chilled or at room temperature. **SERVES 4**

PREP TIME | **20** MINUTES

Here's the perfect dinner solution for evenings when it's too hot to do a lot of cooking. You can substitute leftover or store-bought roasted chicken for the sautéed chicken breasts.

ZUCCHINI AND CHICKEN SALAD

SERVES 4 ■ PREP TIME: 30 MINUTES ■ **TOTAL TIME: 30 MINUTES**

¼ cup plus 1 tablespoon olive oil
¼ cup fresh lemon juice
   Coarse salt and
   fresh ground pepper
1¼ pounds zucchini, thinly sliced
 1 pound boneless,
   skinless chicken breast halves
 1 bunch (8 ounces) spinach,
   chopped
½ red onion, thinly sliced
¾ cup chopped pecans
¼ cup grated Parmesan cheese
¼ cup chopped fresh mint

1 In a large bowl, whisk together ¼ cup of the olive oil, the lemon juice, and salt and pepper to taste. Add the zucchini; toss to coat, and let marinate while cooking the chicken.

2 In a large nonstick skillet, heat the remaining 1 tablespoon olive oil over medium heat. Season the chicken with salt and pepper. Cook until golden brown on both sides, about 7 minutes per side. Remove from the skillet, and slice thin.

3 Toss the chicken with the zucchini mixture, spinach, red onion, pecans, Parmesan cheese, and mint. Serve.

Serve this grilled dinner family-style on a big platter, and let everyone help themselves. You can marinate the chicken up to 30 minutes, if desired.

GARLIC-MARINATED CHICKEN CUTLETS WITH GRILLED POTATOES

SERVES 4 ■ PREP TIME: 30 MINUTES **■ TOTAL TIME: 45 MINUTES**

1½ pounds baby red new potatoes, halved or quartered if large

1 tablespoon plus 1½ teaspoons olive oil, plus more for grates

3 garlic cloves, minced

2 tablespoons white-wine vinegar

1½ tablespoons fresh thyme leaves, chopped, plus sprigs for garnish, if desired

Coarse salt and fresh ground pepper

1½ pounds chicken cutlets (about 6)

1½ pounds medium-thick asparagus, trimmed

1 tablespoon butter

1 tablespoon Garlic Vinaigrette (page 347)

1 Heat a grill to medium. Fold a 4-foot-long sheet of aluminum foil in half to make a double-layer sheet. Place the potatoes on the double layer. Form a packet, folding the foil over the potatoes and crimping the edges to seal. Place on the grill and cook, turning over once, until the potatoes are tender, about 25 minutes. Remove from the heat. Leave the potatoes wrapped in foil to keep warm. Raise the grill to high; lightly oil the grates.

2 Meanwhile, make the marinade: In a large baking dish, whisk together 1 tablespoon of the oil, the garlic, vinegar, thyme, ½ teaspoon salt, and ¼ teaspoon pepper. Add the chicken; turn several times to coat. Let marinate at room temperature for 10 minutes.

3 In a large bowl, toss the asparagus with the remaining 1½ teaspoons oil; season with salt and pepper. Working in batches, if necessary, grill the asparagus, turning occasionally, until lightly browned and tender, 4 to 8 minutes, depending on the thickness of the spears. Set aside.

4 Lift the chicken from the marinade and grill until browned and cooked through, 2 to 3 minutes per side. Remove from the grill. Cover the chicken with foil to keep warm.

5 Remove the warm potatoes from the foil; transfer to a medium bowl, toss with the butter, and season with salt and pepper. Cut the asparagus on the diagonal into 1½-inch pieces. In a medium bowl, toss the asparagus with the vinaigrette. Serve the grilled chicken with the potatoes and asparagus. Garnish with thyme sprigs, if desired.

PREP TIME | **30** MINUTES

Croutons can be made 3 days ahead and stored in a resealable plastic bag, at room temperature. Chicken can be cooked and stored, covered, overnight in the refrigerator. Bring the chicken and dressing to room temperature before serving.

CHICKEN CAESAR SALAD

SERVES 4 ■ PREP TIME: 30 MINUTES ■ **TOTAL TIME: 45 MINUTES**

For the salad

- 4 ounces Italian bread, cut in ¾-inch cubes (about 4 cups)
- 3 tablespoons olive oil
  Coarse salt and fresh ground pepper
- 4 chicken cutlets (each 2 to 3 ounces and ½ inch thick)
- 1 package romaine lettuce hearts (18 to 20 ounces)

For the dressing

- ¼ cup fresh lemon juice
- ¼ cup reduced-fat mayonnaise
- ¼ cup grated Parmesan cheese
- 2 anchovy fillets, coarsely chopped (optional)
- 1 small garlic clove

1 Make the croutons: Preheat the oven to 375°F. Place the bread on a rimmed baking sheet. Drizzle with 2 tablespoons of the oil, and season with salt and pepper; toss to coat. Bake, tossing occasionally, until golden, 12 to 15 minutes. Remove the croutons from the oven and let cool.

2 Make the chicken: Heat the remaining tablespoon oil in a large skillet over high heat. Season the chicken with salt and pepper. Cook until opaque throughout, 1 to 2 minutes per side; remove from the skillet and let cool.

3 Prepare the lettuce: Cut the romaine hearts crosswise into 1-inch ribbons; wash and dry.

4 Make the dressing: In a blender, combine the lemon juice, mayonnaise, Parmesan, anchovy fillets (if using), and garlic; blend until smooth.

5 Slice the chicken crosswise into strips; toss with the croutons, lettuce, and dressing.

Basting the chicken with lemon juice while it's on the grill gives it a tangy taste. For the marinade, steeping the rosemary in hot water intensifies the flavor of the herb.

GRILLED TUSCAN CHICKEN WITH ROSEMARY AND LEMON

SERVES 4 ■ PREP TIME: 30 MINUTES ■ TOTAL TIME: 1 HOUR

2 tablespoons chopped fresh rosemary or 1 tablespoon dried

¼ cup olive oil

2 garlic cloves

Coarse salt and fresh ground pepper

1 (3½- to 4-pound) chicken, cut into 8 or 10 serving pieces

¼ cup fresh lemon juice

1 Heat the grill to medium. In a small saucepan, bring ⅓ cup water and the rosemary to a boil; remove from the heat, cover, and let steep for 5 minutes. Transfer to a blender. Add the oil and garlic; season with salt and pepper. Purée until smooth; let cool.

2 Combine the chicken and the rosemary oil in a shallow dish or resealable plastic bag, and turn to coat. Cover, and let marinate for at least 15 minutes at room temperature or overnight in the refrigerator, turning the chicken occasionally.

3 Remove the chicken from the marinade; place on the grill. Discard the marinade. Cook, basting frequently with the lemon juice and turning as needed to prevent burning, until cooked throughout, 20 to 30 minutes.

GRILLED ZUCCHINI AND SQUASH

2 zucchini (about 1 pound each)

2 yellow squash (about 1 pound each)

2 yellow bell peppers

¼ cup olive oil

Coarse salt and fresh ground pepper

¼ cup thinly sliced basil

Heat the grill to medium. Slice the zucchini and squash into ½-inch-thick slices on the diagonal. Quarter the peppers; remove the seeds and ribs. In a large bowl, toss the vegetables with the olive oil; season with salt and pepper. Grill the vegetables until tender, 6 to 8 minutes per side. Return the vegetables to the bowl; toss with the basil. SERVES 4

In this recipe, cheese and mustard are incorporated into the burger rather than being used as toppings. For juicier burgers, avoid using the leanest ground turkey.

FAVORITE TURKEY BURGER

SERVES 4 ■ PREP TIME: 10 MINUTES ■ **TOTAL TIME: 35 MINUTES**

1½ pounds ground turkey
    (preferably 93 percent lean)
 ½ cup finely grated Gruyère cheese
  4 scallions, thinly sliced
 ¼ cup dried breadcrumbs
 ¼ cup Dijon mustard
  1 garlic clove, minced
    Coarse salt and
    fresh ground pepper
    Vegetable oil, for grates
  4 hamburger buns

Suggested accompaniments
    Cheese slices
    Sliced beefsteak tomatoes
    Red and white onion
    (raw or grilled)
    Ketchup
    Mustard
    Pickles
    Mayonnaise
    Boston lettuce leaves

1 Heat the grill to high. In a medium bowl, use a fork to gently combine the turkey with the Gruyère, scallions, breadcrumbs, Dijon mustard, and garlic; season generously with salt and pepper. Dividing the mixture evenly, gently form the mixture into four 1-inch-thick patties.

2 Lightly oil the grill. Place the patties on the hottest part of the grill; sear until browned, 1 to 2 minutes per side. Move the patties to the cooler part of the grill; continue grilling until cooked through, 5 to 10 minutes per side.

3 Split the hamburger buns and toast on the grill if you like; place a burger on each bun and serve with the desired accompaniments.

The combination of dried spices and fresh seasonings, including lemon, ginger, and scallion, makes these burgers irresistible. Watermelon slices are served on the side to balance the heat of the burgers.

INDIAN-SPICED CHICKEN BURGERS

SERVES 4 ■ PREP TIME: 40 MINUTES ■ **TOTAL TIME: 40 MINUTES**

1½ pounds boneless, skinless chicken thighs (4 to 5), cut into rough chunks

4 scallions, thinly sliced

3 tablespoons chopped fresh ginger (from a peeled 2-inch piece)

2 tablespoons fresh lemon juice

1 tablespoon paprika

2 teaspoons ground cumin

½ teaspoon ground cardamom

¼ teaspoon cayenne pepper

Coarse salt and fresh ground pepper

Vegetable oil, for grates

4 whole-wheat pitas (6-inch)

1 cucumber (8 ounces), halved lengthwise and thinly sliced on the diagonal

½ cup fresh cilantro sprigs

Cumin Yogurt Sauce (recipe below)

Watermelon slices (optional)

1 Heat the grill to medium-high. In a medium bowl, place the chicken, scallions, ginger, lemon juice, paprika, cumin, cardamom, cayenne, 1½ teaspoons coarse salt, and ½ teaspoon pepper; toss to combine. Set aside to marinate for at least 10 and up to 30 minutes.

2 Transfer the chicken mixture to a food processor; pulse until coarsely chopped, but not pasty, 10 to 12 times. Gently form the mixture into sixteen ¾-inch-thick patties (about 3 tablespoons each).

3 Moisten a folded paper towel with oil; grasp with tongs and rub over the grates. Season the patties with salt and pepper; grill until opaque throughout, 2 to 3 minutes per side.

4 Halve the pitas crosswise (toast on the grill, if you like). Into each pocket, place 2 chicken patties, cucumber slices, and cilantro sprigs. Serve with cumin yogurt sauce and, if desired, watermelon slices.

CUMIN YOGURT SAUCE

½ cup plain low-fat yogurt
½ teaspoon ground cumin
Coarse salt and fresh ground pepper

In a small bowl, combine yogurt and cumin; season with salt and pepper.

PREP TIME | **5** MINUTES

Dijon mustard and Worcestershire sauce flavor these burgers before they're cooked. We like them with lettuce, tomato, and mayo on one side, and grilled onions on the other, but try any of the accompaniments listed below.

BEST BEEF BURGERS

SERVES 4 ■ PREP TIME: 5 MINUTES ■ **TOTAL TIME: 25 MINUTES**

2 pounds ground chuck
1 tablespoon Dijon mustard
1 tablespoon Worcestershire sauce
  Coarse salt and
  fresh ground pepper
4 hamburger buns

Suggested accompaniments
  Cheese slices
  Sliced beefsteak tomatoes
  Red and white onions
  (raw or grilled)
  Ketchup
  Mustard
  Pickles
  Mayonnaise
  Boston lettuce leaves

1 Heat the grill to high. In a medium bowl, use a fork to gently combine the ground chuck with the Dijon mustard and Worcestershire sauce; season generously with salt and pepper. Gently form the mixture into four 1-inch-thick patties.

2 Place the patties on the hottest part of the grill; sear until browned, 1 to 2 minutes per side. Move the patties to the cooler part of the grill; continue grilling until desired doneness, 4 to 8 minutes per side.

3 Split the hamburger buns and toast on the grill if you like; place a burger on each bun and serve with the desired accompaniments.

This meal is just right for Father's Day or Fourth of July or any night of the week. Don't be tempted to skip the sauce—like the steak, it takes only 10 minutes to prepare, and the ingredients complement the spices in the steak rub.

SKIRT STEAK WITH SPICY GREEN SALSA

SERVES 4 ■ PREP TIME: 10 MINUTES ■ TOTAL TIME: 30 MINUTES

5 teaspoons chili powder
1½ teaspoons ground cumin
1½ teaspoons dried oregano
   Coarse salt and
   fresh ground pepper
1½ pounds skirt steak
2 teaspoons olive oil, plus more
   for grates

1 In a small bowl, combine the chili powder, cumin, oregano, 1½ teaspoons salt, and ½ teaspoon pepper. Sprinkle the mixture over the steak; drizzle with oil. Let stand, turning to coat evenly with oil halfway through, for 10 minutes.

2 Heat a grill to high; lightly oil the grates. Place the steak on the grill (fold thin end over so steak is an even thickness); cover. Cook, turning once, until the meat has reached the desired doneness, 4 to 6 minutes for medium-rare.

SPICY GREEN SALSA

½ cup fresh cilantro leaves,
   chopped
1 tablespoon minced pickled
   jalapeño chiles
3 tablespoons olive oil
1 teaspoon red-wine vinegar
⅛ teaspoon coarse salt

Combine all ingredients with 1 tablespoon water in a small bowl. The salsa can be refrigerated for 3 to 4 days; cover with plastic wrap, pressing it directly on the surface to prevent discoloration. **MAKES ⅓ CUP**

POTATO SALAD WITH SOUR CREAM AND SCALLIONS

2 pounds white new potatoes,
   quartered and cut into ¾-inch chunks
   Coarse salt and fresh ground pepper
¾ cup reduced-fat sour cream
¼ cup light mayonnaise
½ cup thinly sliced scallions, plus more
   for garnish (optional)
4 slices bacon, cooked and crumbled,
   for garnish (optional)

1 In a large pot, cover the potatoes with salted water. Bring to a boil; reduce the heat. Simmer until the potatoes are tender when pierced with the tip of a sharp paring knife, 12 to 15 minutes. Drain well.

2 Meanwhile, in a large bowl, whisk together the sour cream and mayonnaise; add the warm potatoes, and gently fold to combine. Season with salt and pepper. Cover; refrigerate at least 1 hour and up to 1 day. To serve, season the salad again with salt and pepper; fold in the scallions. Garnish with the bacon and more scallions, if desired. **SERVES 4**

PREP TIME 10 MINUTES

For the neatest, thinnest slices, use a long, thin-bladed slicing or carving knife, and hold the meat in place with tongs while you work.

FLANK STEAK WITH LIME MARINADE

SERVES 4
PREP TIME: 30 MINUTES
TOTAL TIME: 1 HOUR

⅓ cup fresh lime juice (about 4 limes)

2 tablespoons soy sauce

2 scallions, thinly sliced (about ⅓ cup)

2 tablespoons minced peeled fresh ginger

½ teaspoon red pepper flakes

1½ pounds flank steak

Vegetable oil, for grates

Coarse salt and fresh ground pepper

1 In a resealable plastic bag, combine the lime juice, soy sauce, scallions, ginger, and the red pepper. Add the steak and seal the bag (place it in a dish to catch any leaks); marinate the steak in the refrigerator, turning occasionally, for 30 minutes.

2 Heat the grill to high; lightly oil the grates. Remove the steak from the marinade, letting excess drip off (discard the marinade); season with salt and pepper. Place on the grill; cover. Cook, turning once, until the meat has reached the desired doneness, 6 to 8 minutes for medium-rare. Let the steak rest for 10 minutes before slicing thin.

PREP TIME | **10** MINUTES

A traditional Vietnamese sandwich is made with pork, but in this beef variation, the flavors are the same. If you don't want to make steak from scratch, you can use an equal amount of sliced roast beef in its place.

VIETNAMESE STEAK SANDWICHES

SERVES 4 ■ PREP TIME: 10 MINUTES ■ TOTAL TIME: 10 MINUTES

1 large garlic clove, minced

1 teaspoon sugar

¼ teaspoon red pepper flakes

1 tablespoon rice vinegar

2 carrots, grated

2 scallions, thinly sliced

½ cup packed fresh cilantro leaves

4 hero rolls

1 pound sliced Flank Steak with Lime Marinade (page 130)

1 In a small bowl, stir together the garlic, sugar, red pepper flakes, rice vinegar, and 1 tablespoon water.

2 In another bowl, toss together the carrots, scallions, and cilantro leaves. Toss with half the vinegar mixture.

3 Split and lightly toast the hero rolls; dividing evenly, layer with the carrot mixture and steak. Drizzle with the remaining vinegar mixture, if desired.

When buying poblanos, bear in mind that the darker the chile pepper, the richer the flavor, which varies from mild to strong. Roasting the chiles softens them and mellows their spicy flavor.

SKIRT STEAK WITH POBLANO SAUCE

SERVES 4 ■ PREP TIME: 25 MINUTES ■ TOTAL TIME: 25 MINUTES

1½ pounds skirt steak
  1 tablespoon canola oil, plus more for rubbing steak
    Coarse salt and fresh ground pepper
  1 small onion, chopped
  2 garlic cloves, thinly sliced
  1 plum tomato, chopped
  2 poblano chiles, roasted (see note below) and thinly sliced
  1 lime, ½ juiced, ½ cut into wedges

1 Heat the grill to high. Rub the steak with some canola oil; season with salt and pepper. Grill for 3 to 5 minutes per side for medium-rare.

2 Heat the 1 tablespoon canola oil in a medium skillet over medium heat. Add the onion and garlic; cook, stirring often, until golden and fragrant, 3 to 4 minutes. Add the tomato, sliced chiles, lime juice, and ½ to ¾ cup water; season with salt.

3 Reduce the heat; simmer until thickened and saucy, 3 to 5 minutes. Slice the meat; serve with the sauce and lime wedges.

ROASTING CHILE PEPPERS
Roast the pepper over an open flame until charred on all sides, turning as each side blackens. (You can roast directly over a gas burner, on the grill, or on a baking sheet under the broiler.) Fold a paper towel around the chile, and let it steam for 15 to 20 minutes. Using the paper towel to protect your fingers, rub the charred skin off the chile. With a fresh paper towel, split the pepper open lengthwise; remove and discard the seeds and ribs. If your fingers come into contact with the seeds or ribs, wash your hands immediately.

Since both the pork and the salad can be served at room temperature, this is a great make-ahead meal. Prepare it late on a summer evening, once the temperature has dropped, and serve it the next day, when it's too hot to cook. The black-eyed pea salad also pairs well with barbecued chicken.

ROASTED PORK WITH BLACK-EYED PEA SALAD

SERVES 4 ■ PREP TIME: 20 MINUTES ■ **TOTAL TIME: 45 MINUTES**

For the pork
- 1 tablespoon paprika
- 1 teaspoon dried thyme
- ¼ to ½ teaspoon cayenne pepper
- Coarse salt and fresh ground pepper
- 2 pork tenderloins (10 to 12 ounces each)
- 1 tablespoon vegetable oil

For the black-eyed pea salad
- 1 teaspoon Dijon mustard
- 2 tablespoons cider vinegar
- 2 tablespoons vegetable oil
- 1 can (15 ounces) black-eyed peas, drained and rinsed
- 1 package (10 ounces) frozen corn kernels, thawed
- 1 red bell pepper, ribs and seeds removed, finely diced
- 2 scallions, thinly sliced
- Coarse salt and fresh ground pepper

1 Make the pork: Preheat the oven to 450°F. In a small bowl, combine the paprika, thyme, cayenne, 1 teaspoon salt, and ¼ teaspoon pepper; set the spice mixture aside.

2 Place the pork on a rimmed baking sheet; rub with the oil. Sprinkle all over with the spice mixture, patting in gently. Roast until an instant-read thermometer inserted in the thickest part of the meat registers 150°F, 20 to 25 minutes; let cool.

3 Make the black-eyed pea salad: In a medium container, whisk the mustard, vinegar, and oil. Add all the vegetables. Season with salt and pepper; toss to combine.

4 Thinly slice the pork and serve with the salad. The pork and salad can be stored separately in the refrigerator, covered, up to 3 days. Bring both to room temperature, and thinly slice the pork just before serving.

Inspired by the popular Cuban sandwich known as the Cubano, these quesadillas contain many of its signature ingredients—sliced pork, pickles, ham, and cheese.

PORK QUESADILLAS

SERVES 4 ■ PREP TIME: 45 MINUTES ■ **TOTAL TIME: 1 HOUR**

1 large garlic clove, unpeeled
  Coarse salt and
  fresh ground pepper

1 tablespoon vegetable oil, plus
  more for grates

1 pork tenderloin (¾ to 1 pound)

1 large red onion,
  cut into ½-inch-thick slices

4 tablespoons spicy brown mustard, plus more for serving

4 flour tortillas
  (10-inch or burrito-size)

6 ounces thinly sliced baked ham

3 to 4 dill pickles, thinly sliced
  lengthwise

8 ounces provolone or Swiss
  cheese, coarsely shredded
  (about 2 cups)

1 Place the unpeeled garlic clove on a cutting board, and smash with the flat side of a knife blade. Peel off the papery skin and discard; trim away the root end. Holding the tip of the blade steady on the cutting board with your free hand, and rocking the base of the blade back and forth, chop the garlic into coarse, even pieces. Gather the chopped garlic in a pile; sprinkle generously with coarse salt. Place the flat side of the knife blade on top; press firmly, pulling the knife toward you. Repeat until a paste forms. In a small bowl, combine with ¼ teaspoon pepper and the oil. Rub all over the pork.

2 Heat the grill to high; oil the grates. Place the pork on the hottest part of grill; cover. Cook, turning occasionally, until an instant-read thermometer inserted in the thickest part registers 155°F, 10 to 20 minutes. Let rest for 5 minutes; thinly slice the pork across the grain.

3 Meanwhile, place the onion slices on the cooler part of the grill; cover. Cook, turning once, until soft and beginning to brown, about 10 minutes. Reduce the grill to medium-low.

4 Spread 1 tablespoon of the mustard on each tortilla, leaving a ½-inch border. Dividing evenly, layer half of each tortilla with the ham, pork, onion, pickles, and cheese. Fold the tortillas; press to close.

5 Lightly oil the grates again. Place the quesadillas on the grill; cover. Cook, turning once, until browned in spots and the cheese has melted, about 4 minutes. Cut into wedges; serve immediately with additional mustard.

PREP TIME | **45** MINUTES

PREP TIME | **20** MINUTES

In this recipe, lemon wedges caramelize on the grill, making them slightly sweet. When serving the skewers, squeeze the lemon juice over the lamb for added flavor.

LEMON-GARLIC LAMB KEBABS

SERVES 4 ■ PREP TIME: 20 MINUTES ■ **TOTAL TIME: 20 MINUTES**

1½ pounds leg of lamb, well trimmed and cut into 20 equal cubes (about 1 inch each)

8 thin lemon wedges

¼ cup olive oil, plus more for grill

2 tablespoons fresh lemon juice

4 garlic cloves, minced

Coarse salt and ground pepper

Feta Dipping Sauce (recipe below)

Fresh parsley sprigs, for serving (optional)

1 Heat the grill to high. Assemble 4 long skewers, alternating 5 lamb cubes with 2 lemon wedges on each. Arrange the skewers in a nonmetallic dish.

2 In a small bowl, whisk together the oil, lemon juice, and garlic. Pour the marinade over the skewers; turn to coat. Let stand for at least 5 minutes (or cover and refrigerate overnight, turning occasionally). Season with salt and pepper.

3 Lightly oil the grates. Place the skewers on the grill; cover the grill, and cook, turning occasionally, until grill marks are visible and the meat is cooked to the desired doneness, 1 to 2 minutes per side for medium-rare. Serve with the sauce, and garnish with parsley sprigs, if desired.

FETA DIPPING SAUCE

2 ounces feta cheese

1 tablespoon fresh lemon juice

Coarse salt and fresh ground pepper

In a blender, purée the feta, lemon juice, and 2 tablespoons water. Season with salt and ground pepper.

Tzatziki, a traditional Greek dressing made from cucumber, yogurt, and mint, lends a cool complement to the burgers.

GREEK-STYLE MINI LAMB BURGERS

SERVES 4 ■ PREP TIME: 20 MINUTES ■ **TOTAL TIME: 35 MINUTES**

For the tzatziki
- ½ English cucumber, peeled, seeded, and grated (¾ cup)
- ½ cup plain yogurt
- 2 teaspoons fresh lemon juice
- 2 teaspoons chopped fresh mint
- 1 small garlic clove, minced
  Coarse salt and fresh ground pepper

For the lamb burgers
- 1½ pounds ground lamb
- ½ small onion, minced (¼ cup)
- ¼ cup chopped fresh parsley
- 2 teaspoons chopped fresh oregano or 1 teaspoon dried
  Coarse salt and fresh ground pepper
- 4 pita breads (6-inch)
- 2 medium beefsteak tomatoes, sliced, for serving
  Shredded lettuce, for garnish (optional)

1 Heat a grill to high. Make the tzatziki: In a medium bowl, combine the cucumber, yogurt, lemon juice, mint, and garlic; season with salt and pepper. Cover, and refrigerate until ready to use.

2 Make the burgers: In a medium bowl, use a fork to gently combine the lamb, onion, parsley, and oregano; season with salt and pepper. Gently form the mixture into 16 small patties, about ¾ inch thick. Grill until medium-rare, 2 to 3 minutes per side.

3 To serve, warm the pitas on the grill; halve, and fill with the burgers, tzatziki, and tomatoes. Garnish with shredded lettuce, if desired.

PREP TIME | **20** MINUTES

PREP TIME | **30** MINUTES

Filled with Caribbean flavors, this dinner is made to be enjoyed outdoors. You will need twelve metal or wooden skewers. To keep them from scorching on the grill, soak wooden skewers in water while preparing the ingredients.

RUM-GLAZED SHRIMP AND MANGO

SERVES 4 ■ PREP TIME: 30 MINUTES ■ **TOTAL TIME: 45 MINUTES**

¼ cup plus 1 tablespoon fresh lime juice (3 limes)

¼ cup dark rum

3 tablespoons dark brown sugar

1 tablespoon finely grated peeled fresh ginger

1½ teaspoons cornstarch

32 medium shrimp, peeled and deveined (tail on)

Coarse salt and fresh ground pepper

1 ripe but firm mango, peeled and sliced lengthwise into 8 slivers, each about 1 inch thick

2 tablespoons vegetable oil, plus more for grates

2 bunches watercress (about 12 ounces), tough stems trimmed

1 Make glaze: In a small saucepan, combine the ¼ cup lime juice with the rum, sugar, and ginger; bring to a boil over high heat. Reduce the heat; simmer, whisking occasionally, until slightly thickened, about 3 minutes. In a small bowl, whisk together the cornstarch and 1 tablespoon water; stir into the lime-juice mixture. Cook, stirring, until thickened, about 30 seconds. Remove from the heat; let cool.

2 Thread the shrimp onto 8 skewers, using 4 shrimp per skewer. Season on both sides with salt and pepper. Thread the mango slivers onto 4 skewers, using 2 pieces per skewer. Brush the shrimp and mango all over with the reserved glaze.

3 Heat the grill to medium-high; oil the grates. Place the shrimp and mango skewers on the grill; cook, turning once, until blackened in spots and the shrimp are opaque throughout, 3 to 4 minutes.

4 In a large bowl, whisk together the remaining tablespoon lime juice with the 2 tablespoons oil; season with salt and pepper. Add the watercress; toss to coat.

5 To serve, divide the watercress among 4 plates; top each with 2 shrimp skewers and 1 mango skewer.

Experiment with different combinations of your favorite herbs to coat the snapper, but remember to balance strong herbs, such as dill and thyme, with milder ones, such as parsley.

HERB-CRUSTED SNAPPER

SERVES 4 ■ PREP TIME: 15 MINUTES ■ **TOTAL TIME: 30 MINUTES**

1 tablespoon olive oil
4 snapper fillets
(6 to 8 ounces each)
Coarse salt and
fresh ground pepper
2 tablespoons Dijon mustard
½ cup finely chopped assorted
fresh herbs
Couscous, for serving
(optional, recipe on page 359)

1 Preheat the oven to 375°F. Brush a baking sheet with the olive oil. Place the snapper fillets, skin side down, on a work surface; season with salt and pepper and spread each with 1½ teaspoons of the mustard.

2 Place the herbs on a plate; press the mustard-coated side of the fillets in the herbs to coat evenly.

3 Bake the fish on the baking sheet, skin side down, until opaque throughout, 12 to 15 minutes. Serve immediately with couscous, if desired.

Use any salsa you like in this dish: mild, medium, or hot. For the best flavor, buy the fresh variety sold in the refrigerator section of grocery stores. To add more heat, cook ¼ teaspoon red pepper flakes with the corn and garlic in step 3.

CHILI-RUBBED SALMON WITH ZUCCHINI AND SAUTÉED CORN

SERVES 4 ■ PREP TIME: 25 MINUTES ■ **TOTAL TIME: 25 MINUTES**

4 skinless salmon fillets
  (6 ounces each)
  Coarse salt and
  fresh ground pepper
2 teaspoons chili powder
1 pound medium zucchini,
  quartered lengthwise,
  cut crosswise into 3-inch spears
  (about ½ inch thick)
1 tablespoon olive oil
1 package (10 ounces) frozen corn
  kernels (2 cups)
1 garlic clove, minced
½ cup chopped scallions
1 cup prepared fresh tomato salsa
  (half a 12-ounce container)
  Lime wedges, for garnish
  (optional)

1 Heat the broiler; set a rack 4 inches from the heat. Rub the salmon all over with salt and pepper. Arrange on a rimmed baking sheet; sprinkle the top of the fillets with 1 teaspoon of the chili powder. Arrange the zucchini around the salmon; sprinkle with the remaining teaspoon chili powder, and season with salt and pepper.

2 Broil until the fish is opaque throughout and the zucchini is tender, 8 to 10 minutes.

3 Meanwhile, in a large skillet, heat the oil over high heat. Add the corn and garlic; cook, tossing, until the corn is tender and beginning to brown, about 5 minutes. Remove from the heat. Stir in the scallions and salsa; season generously with salt and pepper.

4 Place the fillets on plates, and serve with the zucchini and the corn mixture. Garnish with lime wedges, if desired.

The creamy red-cabbage slaw can also be served on sandwiches or as a side dish. For a toasted flavor, quickly heat the tortillas over a gas burner until blistered in spots, holding each with tongs and waving it from side to side.

FISH TACOS

SERVES 4 ■ PREP TIME: 45 MINUTES ■ TOTAL TIME: 45 MINUTES

¼ cup reduced-fat sour cream
2 tablespoons fresh lime juice
  Coarse salt and
  fresh ground pepper
¼ small red cabbage, thinly
  shredded (about 2½ cups)
4 scallions, thinly sliced
  (about ½ cup)
1 jalapeño chile, halved
  lengthwise, one half minced
2 tablespoons olive oil
1 pound tilapia fillets
  (or other firm white fish),
  cut into 16 equal strips
8 flour tortillas (6-inch)
½ cup fresh cilantro leaves

1 In a large bowl, combine the sour cream and lime juice; season with salt and pepper. Transfer half the mixture to another container; set aside for serving. Toss the cabbage, scallions, and minced jalapeño with the remaining sour-cream mixture. Season again with salt and pepper.

2 In a large nonstick skillet, heat the oil and remaining jalapeño half over medium-high heat; swirl to coat the bottom of the pan. Season the fish on both sides with salt and pepper. In two batches (starting with any larger pieces), cook the fish until golden brown on all sides, 5 to 6 minutes. Discard the jalapeño.

3 Meanwhile, warm the tortillas according to package instructions (or over a burner; see note above).

4 To make the tacos, fill the tortillas with slaw, fish, and fresh cilantro leaves. Drizzle with the reserved sour-cream mixture. Serve immediately.

PREP TIME | **45** MINUTES

Try these spicy vegetarian burgers served on hamburger buns or in whole wheat pita pockets, layered with sliced tomato and red onion and drizzled with tangy yogurt sauce.

LENTIL-WALNUT BURGERS

SERVES 4 ■ PREP TIME: 40 MINUTES ■ **TOTAL TIME: 40 MINUTES**

¾ cup lentils, picked over and rinsed
¾ cup walnuts
⅓ cup plain dried breadcrumbs
3 garlic cloves,
  coarsely chopped
2 teaspoons ground cumin
2 teaspoons ground coriander
¼ to ½ teaspoon red pepper flakes
  Coarse salt and
  fresh ground pepper
4 tablespoons olive oil
1 large egg
  Yogurt-Cilantro Sauce,
  for serving (optional)

YOGURT-CILANTRO SAUCE

¾ cup plain low-fat yogurt
2 tablespoons chopped fresh
  cilantro leaves
1 tablespoon fresh lemon juice
  Coarse salt and
  fresh ground pepper

In a small bowl, whisk together the yogurt, cilantro, and lemon juice; season with salt and pepper.

1 Preheat the oven to 350°F. Place the lentils in a small saucepan, and cover with water by 1 inch. Bring to a boil; reduce to a simmer. Cover, and cook until the lentils are tender but still holding their shape, 15 to 20 minutes. Drain well and cool.

2 Meanwhile, spread the walnuts on a baking sheet, and toast in the oven until fragrant and darkened, about 10 minutes. Let cool.

3 In a food processor, combine the walnuts, breadcrumbs, garlic, cumin, coriander, red pepper flakes, 1½ teaspoons salt, and ¼ teaspoon pepper; process until finely ground. Add the lentils and 1 tablespoon of the oil; pulse until coarsely chopped (some lentils should remain whole).

4 In a large bowl, whisk the egg. Add the lentil mixture; mix well. Divide into 4 equal-size parts; roll into balls, and flatten with the palm of your hand into ¾-inch-thick patties.

5 Heat the remaining 3 tablespoons oil in a large nonstick skillet. Add the burgers; cook over medium-low heat until crisp and browned, turning gently with a thin-edged spatula, 8 to 10 minutes per side. Transfer to a paper-towel-lined plate to drain. Serve with yogurt-cilantro sauce, if desired.

Think of these as open-faced Mexican sandwiches, topped with grilled summer vegetables, tangy feta cheese, and fresh tomato salsa.

GRILLED VEGETABLE TOSTADAS

SERVES 4 ■ PREP TIME: 30 MINUTES ■ TOTAL TIME: 35 MINUTES

3 tablespoons olive oil, plus more for grates

3 medium zucchini (1½ pounds total), cut into ½-inch-wide slices on the diagonal

4 portobello mushrooms (1 pound total), stemmed

1½ bunches scallions, root ends trimmed

Coarse salt and fresh ground pepper

4 flour tortillas (10-inch or burrito-size)

3 cups Fresh Tomato Salsa (recipe below), or store-bought fresh salsa

4 ounces feta cheese, crumbled (1 cup)

1 lime, cut lengthwise into 4 wedges (optional), for serving

1 Heat the grill to high; lightly oil the grates. In separate piles, arrange the zucchini, mushrooms, and scallions on a baking sheet. Drizzle with 2 tablespoons of the oil; season with salt and pepper. Working in batches if necessary, remove each pile of vegetables from the baking sheet. Grill, turning once, until lightly browned and tender, 2 minutes for scallions, 6 minutes for mushrooms, and 8 minutes for zucchini. Return all the vegetables to the baking sheet. Slice the mushrooms into ½-inch-wide strips. Set aside.

2 Brush the tortillas with the remaining tablespoon oil; grill, turning frequently, until browned and very crispy, about 2 minutes. Place 1 tortilla on each serving plate; cover evenly with mushrooms and zucchini. Using kitchen shears, snip scallions over the vegetables. Top with the salsa, and sprinkle with the feta; serve with lime wedges, if desired.

FRESH TOMATO SALSA

1½ pounds plum tomatoes (6 to 8), cored, halved, and seeded

½ medium red onion, minced (½ cup)

1 jalapeño or serrano chile (ribs and seeds removed for less heat, if desired), minced

1 small garlic clove, minced

½ cup chopped fresh cilantro

2 tablespoons fresh lime juice (from 1 lime)

Coarse salt

Chop the tomatoes into ¼-inch pieces; transfer to a medium bowl. Add the onion, chile, garlic, cilantro, and lime juice; season generously with salt. Mix to combine. Let stand 15 minutes to develop flavor. Salsa can be kept at room temperature up to 2 hours. To store, transfer to an airtight container, and refrigerate up to 3 days.

Elegant enough for a dinner party but simple enough to prepare any night of the week, this pasta dish makes good use of quick-cooking shrimp and two types of tomatoes.

SHRIMP, TOMATO, AND BASIL PASTA

SERVES 4 ■ PREP TIME: 30 MINUTES ■ TOTAL TIME: 30 MINUTES

1½ pounds medium shrimp, peeled and deveined (tails removed)

   Coarse salt and fresh ground pepper

6 teaspoons olive oil

2 garlic cloves, minced

1 can (14.5 ounces) diced tomatoes in juice

1 pint cherry or grape tomatoes, halved

½ pound linguine

1½ cups lightly packed fresh basil leaves, torn into small pieces, plus extra leaves for garnish (optional)

1 Season the shrimp with salt and pepper. In a large skillet, heat 4 teaspoons of the oil over high heat. Add the shrimp; cook until opaque throughout, turning occasionally, about 3 minutes. Transfer to a bowl; set aside.

2 Make the sauce: To the same skillet, add the remaining 2 teaspoons oil and the garlic; cook over medium heat until fragrant, about 30 seconds. Add the canned tomatoes and their juice, along with 2 cups water; bring to a boil. Reduce the heat; simmer, stirring occasionally, until the tomatoes have softened and are saucy, about 15 minutes. Remove the sauce from the heat; stir in the cherry tomatoes.

3 Meanwhile, in a large pot of boiling salted water, cook the pasta until al dente according to the package instructions. Drain; return the pasta to the pot. Add the tomato sauce, shrimp, and basil; season with salt and pepper, and toss. Serve immediately, garnished with basil leaves, if desired.

The combination of pesto, potatoes, and green beans originates in Liguria, a region of Italy. It's best made at the height of summer, when fresh basil is readily available, but you can make it any time of year with store-bought pesto.

PASTA WITH PESTO, POTATOES, AND GREEN BEANS

SERVES 4 ■ PREP TIME: 25 MINUTES ■ TOTAL TIME: 40 MINUTES

2 waxy potatoes
  Coarse salt and
  fresh ground pepper
8 ounces cavatappi or other
  short tubular pasta
8 ounces green beans, trimmed
  and halved
½ cup Pesto (recipe page 355)

1 Peel and cut the potatoes into 1-inch cubes; place in a large pot of water and bring to a boil.

2 Add 1 tablespoon salt and the cavatappi; return to a boil and cook for 2 minutes.

3 Add the green beans. Return to a boil; cook until the vegetables are tender and the pasta is al dente according to package instructions.

4 Drain; toss with the pesto and season with salt and pepper. Serve warm or at room temperature.

This is one of the quickest and most satisfying pasta recipes you can make. Prosciutto is easier to slice when it's cold; stack slices, and cut crosswise with a sharp knife.

PASTA WITH PROSCIUTTO AND PEAS

SERVES 4 ■ PREP TIME: 20 MINUTES ■ TOTAL TIME: 20 MINUTES

Coarse salt and
fresh ground pepper

12 ounces fettuccine

1 tablespoon butter

1 large shallot, finely chopped
(¼ cup)

¼ cup heavy cream

1 package (10 ounces) frozen peas,
thawed

8 slices prosciutto (about 4 ounces
total), halved lengthwise
and thinly sliced crosswise
(about 1 cup)

1 tablespoon finely grated
lemon zest

1 tablespoon fresh lemon juice

½ cup finely grated Parmesan
cheese, plus more for serving
(optional)

1 In a large pot of boiling salted water, cook the pasta until al dente according to the package instructions. Reserve 1 cup of the pasta water; drain the pasta and return it to the pot.

2 Meanwhile, make the sauce: In a large skillet, melt the butter over medium-low heat; add the shallot and cook until softened, about 5 minutes. Add the cream, peas, and prosciutlo; bring to a gentle simmer over medium heat. Simmer until the peas are heated through, 3 to 4 minutes.

3 Stir in the lemon zest and juice. Pour the sauce over the pasta; add the Parmesan, and season generously with salt and pepper. Add enough of the reserved pasta water to thin the sauce as desired. Serve immediately; top with additional Parmesan, if desired.

For a delicious appetizer, serve the grilled tomatoes atop toasted pieces of Italian bread. Or use them in a grilled sandwich with fresh mozzarella and basil.

GRILLED TOMATO LINGUINE

SERVES 4 ■ PREP TIME: 25 MINUTES ■ **TOTAL TIME: 45 MINUTES**

3 pounds plum tomatoes, cored and halved lengthwise

5 tablespoons extra-virgin olive oil

1 tablespoon chopped fresh thyme, or 1 teaspoon dried

Coarse salt and fresh ground pepper

1 pound linguine

½ cup finely grated Parmesan cheese, plus more for topping, if desired

1 Heat a grill to high. In a bowl, toss the tomatoes with 3 tablespoons of the olive oil and the thyme; season generously with salt and pepper.

2 Starting with cut sides down, grill the tomatoes until soft and charred, 8 to 12 minutes per side.

3 Return to the bowl; cut into coarse pieces with kitchen shears.

4 Meanwhile, cook the linguine in a large pot of boiling salted water until al dente according to the package instructions. Drain; return to the pot.

5 Add the remaining 2 tablespoons extra-virgin olive oil, the Parmesan, and grilled tomatoes. Divide among bowls, and serve immediately with more grated Parmesan, if desired.

Customize this toss-and-serve pasta dish by adding any—
or all—of the suggested toppings.

RIGATONI WITH GOAT CHEESE

SERVES 4 TO 6 ■ PREP TIME: 10 MINUTES ■ **TOTAL TIME: 25 MINUTES**

Coarse salt and
fresh ground pepper
1 pound rigatoni
1½ cups crumbled goat cheese
(about 4 ounces)
½ cup finely grated Parmesan
cheese

Topping suggestions
¼ cup sliced pitted black olives
¼ cup chopped or torn herbs
¼ cup toasted pine nuts
(see page 275)
¼ cup slivered sun-dried tomatoes

1 In a large pot of boiling salted water, cook the rigatoni until al dente according to the package directions; drain, reserving ½ cup of the cooking water.

2 Return the pasta to the pot, and toss with the goat cheese and Parmesan cheese. Season with salt and pepper, and add some of the reserved pasta water as desired.

3 Sprinkle the pasta with any or all of the suggested toppings, as desired, and serve immediately.

Once you learn to cook corn on the grill, it may become your favorite way to prepare it. Don't skip the chili powder or paprika here; it really heightens the smoky flavor of the grilled corn.

GRILLED CORN ON THE COB

SERVES 4 ■ PREP TIME: 15 MINUTES ■ TOTAL TIME: 25 MINUTES

4 ears corn
   Vegetable oil, for grates
1 tablespoon butter, cut into 4 pats
   Coarse salt and
   fresh ground pepper
   Chili powder or paprika

1 Peel back the corn husks, leaving them attached at the base of the ear. Remove and discard the silk; pull the husks back over the corn. Place the ears in a large bowl or pot; cover with cold water. Let soak for 10 minutes.

2 Preheat the grill to high; lightly oil the grates. Drain the corn. Arrange the ears on the grill. Cover and cook, turning occasionally, using tongs, until the husks are slightly charred and the corn is tender, 15 to 20 minutes. Remove the ears from the grill. Holding the bottom of each hot ear with a towel, peel back the husks and, with a knife, coat the kernels with butter. Season the corn with salt, pepper, and chili powder or paprika. Serve immediately.

PREP TIME **15** MINUTES

Since the corn is not cooked for the salad, it's important to use the freshest you can find, preferably from a roadside stand or farmers' market. Serve the fritters warm, topped with dollops of cool sour cream.

CORN SALAD

SERVES 4 ■ PREP TIME: 15 MINUTES ■ TOTAL TIME: 15 MINUTES

6 ears corn, husks and silk removed
3 scallions, thinly sliced crosswise (½ cup)
2 tablespoons white-wine vinegar
2 tablespoons olive oil
  Coarse salt and fresh ground pepper

1 To remove the kernels, cut off the tip of each cob; stand the cob in a wide shallow bowl. With a sharp knife, slice downward to remove the kernels.

2 To the bowl, add the scallions, vinegar, and oil. Season generously with salt and pepper; toss to combine. Serve, or cover and refrigerate up to 1 day.

CORN FRITTERS

SERVES 4 ■ PREP TIME: 20 MINUTES ■ TOTAL TIME: 20 MINUTES

3 ears corn, husks and silk removed
⅓ cup milk
1 large egg
1 teaspoon sugar
½ teaspoon baking powder
  Coarse salt and fresh ground pepper
¼ cup cornmeal
¼ cup flour
2 tablespoons vegetable oil
  Sour cream (optional)

1 Preheat the oven to 200°F. To remove the kernels, cut off the tip of each cob; stand the cob in a wide shallow bowl. With a sharp knife, slice downward to remove the kernels.

2 To the bowl, add the milk, egg, sugar, baking powder, ½ teaspoon salt, and ¼ teaspoon pepper; mix. Fold in the cornmeal and flour.

3 Line a rimmed baking sheet with paper towels. In a large nonstick skillet, heat 1 tablespoon of the oil over medium heat. Working in two batches, drop the batter into the pan by heaping tablespoonfuls. Fry until golden brown, about 2 minutes per side. Transfer to the prepared baking sheet. Sprinkle with salt; place in the oven. Repeat. Keep warm in the oven for up to 30 minutes. Serve with sour cream, if desired.

BOK CHOY, CARROT, AND APPLE SLAW

1 pound baby bok choy (4 to 6 heads), halved lengthwise
    Coarse salt and fresh ground pepper
1 apple, peeled and cut into matchsticks
2 large carrots, shredded
3 tablespoons fresh lemon juice
1 tablespoon vegetable oil
1 teaspoon finely grated peeled fresh ginger

1 Rinse the bok choy under cold water to remove grit. Cut crosswise into thin strips; place in a large colander, and sprinkle with 1 teaspoon salt. Toss to coat. Top with a plate that fits inside the colander; weight with a heavy object (such as a skillet or canned goods). Set aside in sink to drain.

2 In a large bowl, mix apple, carrots, lemon juice, oil, and ginger. Add bok choy; season with salt and pepper. Toss. **SERVES 4**

SAUTÉED ZUCCHINI, PEPPERS, AND TOMATOES

1 pound zucchini (about 2 medium)
2 yellow bell peppers, ribs and seeds removed
2 tablespoons olive oil
1 pint grape tomatoes
2 garlic cloves, smashed
    Coarse salt and fresh ground pepper

1 Quarter the zucchini lengthwise; cut crosswise into ½-inch-thick pieces. Cut the peppers into ¾-inch squares.

2 Heat the olive oil in a large skillet over medium-high heat. Add the zucchini, peppers, tomatoes, and garlic; season with salt and pepper. Cook, tossing frequently, until the vegetables are crisp-tender, 6 to 8 minutes. **SERVES 4**

JICAMA SLAW

1½ pounds jicama (1 medium), peeled and julienned
½ small red onion, halved and thinly sliced
¼ cup coarsely chopped fresh cilantro
2 to 3 tablespoons fresh lime juice (from 1 to 2 limes)
    Coarse salt and fresh ground pepper

In a medium bowl, place the jicama, onion, cilantro, and lime juice. Season with salt and pepper; toss gently to combine. Serve immediately, or cover and refrigerate for up to 6 hours. **SERVES 4**

GRILLED SWEET POTATOES WITH SCALLIONS

3 sweet potatoes, peeled and cut lengthwise into ½-inch-thick slices
3 tablespoons olive oil
1 teaspoon dried thyme
¼ teaspoon cayenne pepper
    Coarse salt and fresh ground pepper
2 tablespoons butter
2 scallions, thinly sliced

1 Heat a grill to medium. Toss the sweet potatoes in a large bowl with the olive oil, thyme, and cayenne pepper; season with salt and pepper.

2 Grill the potatoes, turning frequently, until tender when pierced with the tip of a paring knife, 20 to 30 minutes.

3 Return the grilled potatoes to the bowl; add the butter, and break the potatoes into large pieces with the side of a spoon. Toss in the scallions, and serve. **SERVES 4**

Here's a clever idea for serving store-bought ice cream. The snowballs are especially fun for children. You will need 1½ cups of topping total. Use toffee chips straight from the bag, or crush up your own favorite candies.

SUMMER SNOWBALLS

SERVES 4 ■ PREP TIME: 15 MINUTES ■ TOTAL TIME: 1 HOUR

1½ pints vanilla ice cream

Suggested toppings
    Toffee chips
    Sweetened shredded coconut
    Sliced almonds

1 Preheat the oven to 350°F if using coconut or almonds. Spread the coconut and/or almonds on a rimmed baking sheet and toast in the oven, tossing occasionally, for 8 to 10 minutes. Transfer to a plate, and let cool completely before using.

2 Tightly cover a baking dish with plastic wrap, stretching it over the top (this will prevent the snowballs from flattening on the bottom.) With an ice-cream scoop, form vanilla ice cream into 8 balls, dipping the scoop in hot water as you work and dropping the balls onto the prepared dish. Freeze until firm, about 30 minutes.

3 One at a time, remove the balls from the freezer, roll in the desired topping, and return to the freezer. Freeze until set, at least 10 minutes and up to 2 days, before serving.

PREP TIME | **15** MINUTES

PREP TIME | **15** MINUTES

You may not have thought of cooking peaches before, but they are delicious hot off the grill and topped with dollops of sweetened sour cream and crumbled cookies.

GRILLED PEACHES WITH SWEETENED SOUR CREAM

SERVES 4 ■ PREP TIME: 15 MINUTES ■ TOTAL TIME: 15 MINUTES

4 peaches, halved and pitted
2 tablespoons melted unsalted butter
½ cup sour cream
1 tablespoon light brown sugar
1 cup crushed amaretti cookies

1 Heat a grill to medium-low. Brush both sides of the peaches with some butter.

2 Place the peaches on the grill; cover the grill, and cook until the peaches are charred and softened, 4 to 5 minutes per side. Set aside.

3 In a small bowl, whisk together the sour cream and sugar.

4 Spoon the mixture over the peaches; sprinkle with the crushed cookies.

A ginger-infused simple syrup flavors slices of store-bought pound cake in this easy but spectacular summer dessert. The recipe is versatile: feel free to substitute other berries, or try slices of peaches, plums, or apricots.

BLACKBERRY AND GINGER TRIFLE

SERVES 8
PREP TIME: 30 MINUTES
TOTAL TIME: 1 HOUR

1 piece (3 inches) fresh ginger, peeled and coarsely chopped

¾ cup sugar

1 store-bought pound cake (12 to 16 ounces)

2 cups heavy cream, chilled

2 packages (6 ounces each) fresh blackberries

1 In a small saucepan, combine the ginger, ½ cup of the sugar, and ½ cup water. Bring to a boil, stirring until the sugar dissolves. Cover the pan and remove from heat; set aside to steep for at least 20 minutes and up to 1 hour. (The longer the syrup steeps, the stronger the ginger flavor will be.)

2 With a serrated knife, cut the pound cake into 1-inch-thick slices; lay the slices on a piece of wax paper (for easier cleanup). With a brush, dab the slices on both sides with the syrup, leaving chopped ginger behind; use all the syrup. Cut the slices into cubes.

3 Whip the cream with the remaining ¼ cup sugar until soft peaks form. In alternating layers, arrange the cake cubes, whipped cream, and blackberries in 8 serving glasses or dishes (or one large, deep serving dish, preferably glass). Chill until ready to serve, at least 30 minutes and up to overnight.

Not only is this one of the simplest desserts to prepare—
it's also low in calories and virtually fat-free. Because it is so
light and refreshing, it's a perfect ending to a heavy meal.

CANTALOUPE WITH HONEY AND LIME

SERVES 4 ■ PREP TIME: 10 MINUTES ■ **TOTAL TIME: 10 MINUTES**

1 cantaloupe, peeled and seeded
¼ cup honey
Finely grated zest and juice
of 1 lime

1 Using a sharp knife, slice the cantaloupe as thin as possible. Mound the slices on 4 serving plates, dividing evenly.

2 Drizzle the cantaloupe with the honey, and then sprinkle with lime zest and juice. Serve immediately.

HOW TO SLICE A MELON
1 Using a sharp knife, slice off the top and bottom of the melon so that it sits flat on a work surface.

2 Following the shape of the melon, slice off the peel in strips, from top to bottom.

3 Halve the peeled melon lengthwise, and scrape out the seeds with a spoon before slicing.

Often reserved for breakfast, crumb is just as satisfying when served for dessert. Replace the blueberries with other berries or sliced apples or plums, if desired.

BLUEBERRY CRUMB CAKE

SERVES 9 ■ PREP TIME: 20 MINUTES ■ TOTAL TIME: 1 HOUR 10 MINUTES

4 tablespoons unsalted butter, at room temperature, plus more for pan

1½ cups all-purpose flour, plus more for pan and 1 teaspoon for blueberries

1½ teaspoons baking powder

½ teaspoon baking soda

¼ teaspoon salt

¼ teaspoon ground allspice

¾ cup sugar

1 large egg

¼ cup buttermilk

1½ cups blueberries, picked over, rinsed, and patted dry

Streusel Topping (recipe follows)

1 Preheat the oven to 350°F. Butter a 9-inch square baking pan; dust with flour, tapping out excess.

2 In a medium bowl, whisk together the 1½ cups flour, the baking powder, baking soda, salt, and allspice. In another bowl, cream the butter and sugar with an electric mixer until light and fluffy. Add the egg; beat until combined.

3 Add the flour mixture and buttermilk in alternating batches, beginning and ending with the flour; beat until just combined (the batter will be very stiff).

4 In a small bowl, toss the blueberries with the remaining teaspoon flour. Fold the berries into the batter; pour into the prepared pan. Sprinkle evenly with the streusel topping, covering the batter completely (do not press in). Bake until golden brown and a toothpick inserted in the center comes out clean, 45 to 50 minutes. Let cool completely.

STREUSEL TOPPING

1 cup all-purpose flour

½ cup packed light brown sugar

¼ teaspoon salt

½ cup (1 stick) cold unsalted butter, cut into tablespoons

In a medium bowl, mix the flour, sugar, and salt. Using your fingers, work in the butter until large, moist crumbs form. (Make sure the crumbs are large so they form a crisp topping as the cake bakes instead of melting into the batter.) Chill streusel until ready to use.

PREP TIME | **20** MINUTES

FALL

FALL SIGNALS A RETURN TO THE KITCHEN, as the days ease back into a regular routine and we begin spending more time inside. There's still an abundance of fresh fruits and vegetables, but they're heartier than their summer counterparts and able to stand up to longer cooking techniques, such as braising, roasting, and caramelizing.

Some of these dinners may take longer from start to finish, but they require less preparation time. Roasting usually involves nothing more than tossing ingredients with a little oil and a few seasonings, then letting the heat of the oven do the rest of the work, bringing out intense flavor in the process. Braising requires cooking in liquid at a slow simmer, which produces wonderfully moist dishes. And caramelizing fruit or vegetables is a browning process that results in an accumulation of extra flavor.

Fall also sees a return to more substantial sauces for pasta, along with sandwiches with a back-to-school feel—think sloppy Joes and fish po'boys. Desserts are rustic and homey, relying as they do on autumn favorites such as pears or apples baked atop an easy pastry base, and stone fruits simply roasted, with fresh herbs as embellishment.

Substitute other available squashes or even pumpkin if you can't find butternut. Toss leftover spicy pumpkin seeds into a salad, or enjoy them on their own as a snack.

PURÉED BUTTERNUT SQUASH SOUP

SERVES 4 ■ PREP TIME: 25 MINUTES ■ TOTAL TIME: 45 MINUTES

2 tablespoons butter

1 small onion, chopped

1 piece (2 inches) peeled fresh ginger, chopped

2 garlic cloves, chopped

2¾ pounds small butternut squash, peeled, seeds removed, and flesh cut into ¾-inch cubes

¼ cup fresh orange juice

Coarse salt and fresh ground pepper

Sour cream (optional)

Spicy Pumpkin Seeds (optional; recipe below)

1 Melt the butter in a large saucepan over medium heat. Cook the onion until fragrant, about 2 minutes. Add the ginger, garlic, and squash; cook, stirring occasionally, until fragrant, 6 to 8 minutes. Stir in 4 cups water. Bring to a boil; reduce the heat. Simmer until the squash is tender, about 20 minutes.

2 Purée the soup in two batches. Stir in the orange juice and 1½ teaspoons salt. Serve hot, with sour cream, pepper, and pumpkin seeds, if desired.

PURÉEING SOUP
When blending hot foods, allow the heat to escape to prevent spattering. Remove the cap from the hole of the blender's lid, and cover the hole with a dish towel while blending.

SPICY PUMPKIN SEEDS

1 cup raw green pumpkin seeds

1 teaspoon chili powder

⅛ to ¼ teaspoon cayenne pepper

½ teaspoon coarse salt

2 teaspoons fresh lime juice

Preheat the oven to 350°F. In a medium bowl, combine all the ingredients and toss to coat. Spread on a rimmed baking sheet; bake until puffed and browned, about 10 minutes.

With fresh ginger, garlic, and lime, this Thai-style soup imparts lovely fragrance and warmth on a cool autumn evening. Adjust the amount of red pepper flakes depending on how spicy you want the soup to be.

COCONUT SHRIMP SOUP

SERVES 4 ■ PREP TIME: 30 MINUTES ■ **TOTAL TIME: 30 MINUTES**

1 tablespoon vegetable oil

1 tablespoon grated peeled fresh ginger

2 garlic cloves, minced

¼ to ½ teaspoon red pepper flakes

1 pound carrots (6 to 8 medium), peeled, halved lengthwise, and thinly sliced

1 can (13.5 ounces) coconut milk

1 tablespoon cornstarch

4 ounces angel hair pasta

1½ pounds large shrimp, peeled, deveined, and tails removed

¼ cup fresh lime juice

Coarse salt

4 scallions, thinly sliced

1 Heat the oil in a large (3-quart) saucepan over medium-low heat. Add the ginger, garlic, and the pepper flakes; cook, stirring, until fragrant, about 1 minute. Add the carrots, coconut milk, and 3 cups water. In a small bowl, mix the cornstarch and 2 tablespoons water until smooth; add to the pot. Bring to a boil.

2 Break the pasta in half; add to the pot. Return to a boil, reduce the heat to medium, and simmer until the pasta is al dente and the carrots are just tender, 3 to 4 minutes.

3 Add the shrimp; stir until opaque, about 1 minute. Remove the pot from the heat and stir in the lime juice; season with salt. Ladle into serving bowls, and garnish with the scallions. Serve immediately.

Oats lend an interesting texture to this soup, but because they are added in such a small quantity and are puréed with the rest of the ingredients, they're impossible to detect.

CREAMY BROCCOLI SOUP

SERVES 4 ■ PREP TIME: 15 MINUTES ■ TOTAL TIME: 30 MINUTES

1 tablespoon olive oil

1 medium onion, halved and sliced

⅛ teaspoon ground nutmeg

4 cups reduced-sodium chicken broth

⅓ cup rolled oats

1½ pounds broccoli, florets separated, stems peeled and cut into ½-inch rounds

Coarse salt and fresh ground pepper

1 In a large saucepan, heat the olive oil over medium-low heat. Add the onion; cook until softened, 5 minutes. Add the nutmeg; cook until fragrant, 30 seconds.

2 Stir in the chicken broth, 1½ cups water, the oats, and broccoli. Season with salt and pepper. Bring to a boil; reduce the heat. Simmer until the broccoli is tender, 5 to 10 minutes.

3 Purée the soup in batches, filling the blender halfway (see note on page 185). Return the soup to the pot, and season with salt and pepper. Serve immediately.

Large, with a firm, sweet flesh, Fujis are good for snacking, cooking, and mixing into salads like this one. Unlike many other apples, their taste actually improves with age.

APPLE, ENDIVE, AND GRAPE SALAD

SERVES 6 ■ PREP TIME: 25 MINUTES ■ **TOTAL TIME: 25 MINUTES**

¼ cup reduced-fat sour cream

¼ cup low-fat buttermilk

2 tablespoons cider vinegar
Coarse salt and
fresh ground pepper

2 Fuji apples,
cored and thinly sliced

1½ pounds Belgian endives (4 to 6),
halved lengthwise, trimmed, and
cut crosswise into 1-inch pieces

2 cups seedless green grapes,
halved lengthwise

½ cup toasted pecans, broken
into pieces

1 In a large bowl, whisk together the sour cream, buttermilk, and vinegar; season generously with salt and pepper.

2 Cut the apple slices in half crosswise; add to the bowl along with the endives, grapes, and pecans. Toss to combine. Serve immediately.

PREP TIME | **15** MINUTES

Try this slightly spicy salad with roast pork or chicken. Shredding the vegetables in a food processor makes the preparation lightning fast; you can shred them on a four-sided box grater instead, but it will increase the prep and total times.

SHREDDED BEET AND CARROT SALAD

SERVES 6 ■ PREP TIME: 15 MINUTES ■ **TOTAL TIME: 15 MINUTES**

¼ cup fresh lemon juice
1 tablespoon extra-virgin olive oil
1 tablespoon honey
¾ teaspoon ground cumin
½ teaspoon ground coriander
¼ teaspoon ground cinnamon
⅛ to ¼ teaspoon cayenne pepper
Coarse salt
1 pound raw beets, peeled
2 carrots, peeled
⅓ cup coarsely torn fresh parsley

1 In a medium bowl, whisk together the lemon juice, oil, honey, cumin, coriander, cinnamon, cayenne, and ¾ teaspoon salt.

2 In a food processor fitted with the shredding disk, shred the beets and then the carrots. Add to the bowl along with the parsley, and toss all of the ingredients to combine.

This simply dressed assortment of wholesome vegetables and legumes is full of bright color, texture, and flavor. Serve it as a starter or side at dinner, and save any leftovers for lunch the next day.

BROCCOLI, CHICKPEA, AND TOMATO SALAD

SERVES 6 ■ PREP TIME: 20 MINUTES ■ **TOTAL TIME: 20 MINUTES**

1 pound broccoli
1 tablespoon Dijon mustard
2 tablespoons red-wine vinegar
2 tablespoons olive oil
½ small red onion, minced
   Coarse salt and
   fresh ground pepper
1 pint cherry tomatoes, halved
1 can (15 ounces) chickpeas,
   drained and rinsed

1 Cut the florets from the broccoli (reserve the stalks for another use). In a large pot fitted with a steamer basket, bring 1 inch of water to a boil. Add the broccoli in a single layer. Cover; steam until crisp-tender, about 5 minutes.

2 In a large bowl, whisk together the mustard, vinegar, olive oil, and onion; season with salt and pepper.

3 Add the tomatoes, chickpeas, and broccoli; toss to coat. Serve chilled or at room temperature.

Using canned beets keeps the prep time to a minimum, but you can substitute roasted beets if you wish (see note below).

ARUGULA, BEET, AND GOAT-CHEESE SALAD

SERVES 4 ■ PREP TIME: 20 MINUTES ■ **TOTAL TIME: 20 MINUTES**

½ cup walnuts

1 tablespoon finely chopped shallot

2 tablespoons red-wine vinegar

2 tablespoons fresh orange juice

3 tablespoons olive oil

Coarse salt and fresh ground pepper

1 can (15 ounces) whole beets, drained and sliced into ½-inch wedges

6 ounces soft goat cheese, at room temperature

8 ounces (1 bunch) arugula, stemmed and washed well

2 ounces (4 cups) frisée

1 Scatter the walnuts on a baking sheet; toast in a 350°F oven, tossing once, until golden brown and fragrant, about 10 minutes. Let cool, then finely chop and place in a shallow dish.

2 In a small bowl, whisk together the shallot, vinegar, orange juice, and oil; season with salt and pepper. Place the beets in a small bowl. Pour one third of the dressing over the beets; toss to coat.

3 With your hands, form the goat cheese into 12 equal balls. Roll the balls one at a time in the walnuts, turning to coat completely, then gently press with fingers to flatten into disks.

4 Place the arugula in a large bowl. Tear the frisée into large pieces, and add to the bowl. Drizzle the greens with the remaining dressing, and toss to combine. Divide among 4 plates, and top each serving with some of the sliced beets and 3 goat-cheese disks.

ROASTING BEETS
To roast, wrap 1 pound (about 5) small, well-scrubbed beets in 2 or 3 packets of foil; place on a baking sheet, and bake in a preheated 450°F oven until the beets are slightly soft to the touch, 45 minutes to 1 hour depending on their size. Cool the beets in the packets, then rub off the skins.

For a break from roast chicken, try these smaller hens, which cook in about half the time it takes for a chicken. If you like, substitute four bone-in, skin-on chicken breasts (10 to 12 ounces each) for the Cornish hens.

ROASTED CORNISH HENS WITH GRAPES

SERVES 4 ■ PREP TIME: 15 MINUTES ■ TOTAL TIME: 50 MINUTES

1½ pounds mixed red and green seedless grapes

8 shallots, root end intact, halved if large

6 sprigs thyme, plus additional leaves for hens

2 tablespoons olive oil

Coarse salt and fresh ground pepper

4 Cornish game hens (1 to 1¼ pounds each)

1 Preheat the oven to 450°F. On a rimmed baking sheet, toss the grapes and shallots with the thyme sprigs, olive oil, 1 teaspoon salt, and ¼ teaspoon pepper.

2 Tie the legs with kitchen twine; nestle the hens among the grapes on the baking sheet, breast side up. Season the hens generously with salt and pepper; sprinkle with thyme leaves.

3 Roast, basting the hens occasionally with the pan juices, until an instant-read thermometer inserted in thickest part of the leg (avoiding the bone) registers 160°F, 30 to 35 minutes.

PREP TIME 15 MINUTES

Browning the chicken seals in the juices and keeps the inside moist and flavorful. This recipe can be made with pork cutlets instead of chicken. For an earthier flavor, substitute shiitake, cremini, or wild mushrooms for the white mushrooms.

BRAISED CHICKEN WITH MUSHROOMS AND OVEN-BAKED POLENTA

SERVES 4 ▪ PREP TIME: 30 MINUTES ▪ TOTAL TIME: 55 MINUTES

4 boneless, skinless chicken breast halves (6 ounces each)
  Coarse salt and fresh ground pepper
2 tablespoons olive oil
1 pound white mushrooms, wiped clean and sliced ½ inch thick
4 garlic cloves, halved
½ cup dry white wine (optional)
1¾ cups reduced-sodium chicken broth
2 tablespoons chopped fresh parsley, plus more for garnish
  Oven-Baked Polenta (recipe below)

1 Sprinkle the chicken breasts with ¼ teaspoon each salt and pepper. Heat 1 tablespoon of the oil in a large skillet over high heat. Add the chicken; cook until lightly browned, 2 to 3 minutes per side. Transfer to a plate.

2 Add the remaining tablespoon oil to the hot skillet. Add the mushrooms, garlic, and ¼ teaspoon salt. Cover; cook over medium heat until the mushrooms release their juices, 2 to 3 minutes. Remove the lid. Cook over high heat, tossing occasionally, until the mushrooms are golden, 4 to 5 minutes.

3 Pour the wine, if using, into the skillet; cook, stirring, until evaporated, 1 minute. Add the stock and parsley; cook over medium-high heat until the mushrooms are tender and the liquid has reduced, 8 to 10 minutes.

4 Return the chicken to the skillet. Cover; simmer over low heat until the chicken is cooked through, 10 to 12 minutes. Serve the cutlets and polenta topped with the mushrooms and a drizzle of cooking liquid. Garnish with additional fresh parsley.

OVEN-BAKED POLENTA

¾ cup cornmeal
  Coarse salt and fresh ground pepper
¼ cup milk
2 tablespoons butter
1 teaspoon fresh marjoram (or ¼ teaspoon dried)

1 Preheat the oven to 425°F. In a lidded baking dish, whisk together 3 cups water, the cornmeal, 1¼ teaspoons salt, and ⅛ teaspoon pepper. Cover, and bake for 30 minutes, stirring halfway through.

2 Remove from the oven, and add the milk, butter, and marjoram, and whisk briskly until smooth. Serve immediately.
SERVES 4

Wrapping the stir-fried chicken in lettuce keeps this dish lower in calories and carbohydrates than it would be if served with tortillas. You could omit the lettuce and serve the chicken over rice, if desired.

CHICKEN STIR-FRY WRAPS

SERVES 4 ■ PREP TIME: 30 MINUTES ■ **TOTAL TIME: 45 MINUTES**

1½ pounds boneless, skinless chicken breast halves, halved horizontally and thinly sliced

Coarse salt and fresh ground pepper

2 tablespoons olive oil

1 large onion, halved and thinly sliced

1 large red bell pepper, ribs and seeds removed, thinly sliced

3 garlic cloves, minced

1½ teaspoons grated peeled fresh ginger

¼ to ½ teaspoon red pepper flakes

3 tablespoons soy sauce

3 tablespoons rice vinegar

1½ teaspoons cornstarch mixed with 1 tablespoon water

12 to 16 Boston lettuce leaves (about 2 heads)

1 Season the chicken with salt and pepper. In a large nonstick skillet, heat 1 tablespoon of the oil over high heat. Add half the chicken; cook, stirring constantly, until opaque throughout, 2 to 4 minutes. Transfer to a plate. Repeat with the remaining chicken.

2 Add the remaining tablespoon oil to the pan, along with the onion and bell pepper. Cook, stirring constantly, until the onion is tender and golden, about 4 minutes (reduce the heat if browning too quickly).

3 Reduce the heat to medium; add the garlic, ginger, and red pepper flakes to the pan; cook, stirring, until fragrant, 30 to 60 seconds.

4 Stir in the soy sauce, vinegar, and cornstarch mixture; remove from the heat. Add the chicken and any accumulated juices; toss to coat. Serve in lettuce cups.

This dish may sound spicy, but roasting the poblano chile and combining it with cream actually mellows its flavor and heat. Serve with white rice mixed with chopped fresh cilantro and scallions on the side.

CHICKEN WITH POBLANO CREAM SAUCE

SERVES 4 ■ PREP TIME: 15 MINUTES ■ TOTAL TIME: 25 MINUTES

1 poblano chile
2 tablespoons canola oil
½ small onion, chopped
1 garlic clove, minced
⅓ cup heavy cream
Coarse salt and fresh ground pepper
4 boneless, skinless chicken breast halves (6 ounces each)

1 Roast the chile over a gas burner or under the broiler, until charred all over. Wrap in a paper towel; steam for 5 minutes. Rub off the skin; remove the seeds and ribs. Chop coarsely.

2 Heat 1 tablespoon of the canola oil in a small saucepan over medium heat; add the onion and garlic; cook until soft, 5 to 7 minutes. Add the chile and cream.

3 Purée in a blender; add water if too thick. Season with salt and pepper.

4 Season the chicken with salt and pepper. Heat the remaining tablespoon canola oil in a large skillet over medium-high heat. Cook the chicken until it is golden and the juices run clear, 4 to 5 minutes per side. Serve with the sauce.

To complete the meal, add a side of spaghetti or other pasta tossed with a little olive oil and some grated Parmesan cheese, and seasoned with salt and pepper.

PARMESAN-STUFFED CHICKEN BREASTS

SERVES 4
PREP TIME: 10 MINUTES
TOTAL TIME: 45 MINUTES

1 cup fresh flat-leaf parsley leaves, chopped

¼ cup plain dried breadcrumbs

¼ cup grated Parmesan cheese

Grated zest of 1 lemon (about 1 tablespoon)

Coarse salt and fresh ground pepper

4 bone-in chicken breast halves (about 3 pounds)

---

1 Preheat the oven to 450°F. In a small bowl, mix the parsley, breadcrumbs, Parmesan, and zest. Season the mixture with ¼ teaspoon each salt and pepper.

2 Divide the parsley mixture into 4 mounds. Carefully loosen the chicken skin with fingers; tuck the parsley mixture under the skin. Season the chicken with salt and pepper. Place in a 9-by-13-inch roasting pan.

3 Bake until the skin is crispy, the chicken is cooked through, and an instant-read thermometer inserted in the thickest part of the meat registers 165°F, about 30 minutes.

PREP TIME | **10** MINUTES

Mushrooms, acorn squash, and rosemary lend a woodsy taste to roast chicken. We used cremini mushrooms, but regular white button mushrooms can be substituted.

ROASTED CHICKEN AND VEGETABLES

SERVES 4 ■ PREP TIME: 10 MINUTES ■ **TOTAL TIME: 1 HOUR**

1 acorn squash, halved lengthwise, seeded, and sliced ½ inch thick

1 pound cremini mushrooms, trimmed and halved

1 large red onion, cut into ½-inch wedges

8 garlic cloves, crushed

1 tablespoon olive oil

Coarse salt and fresh ground pepper

4 bone-in chicken breast halves (10 ounces each)

1 tablespoon dried rosemary, crumbled

1 Preheat the oven to 375°F. Combine the squash, mushrooms, onion, garlic, and oil in a roasting pan; season with salt and pepper, and toss to coat. Roast until the squash is beginning to soften and all the vegetables are heated through, about 15 minutes.

2 Meanwhile, lift up the skin from the chicken breasts; rub the flesh with the rosemary and some salt and pepper. Replace the skin; season the chicken all over with more salt.

3 Remove the roasting pan from the oven, and place the chicken, skin sides up, on top of the vegetables. Return to the oven; continue roasting until the chicken is cooked through and the vegetables are tender, about 35 minutes.

PREPARING ACORN SQUASH
Wash, dry, and halve the squash lengthwise; scoop out the seeds with a spoon, then slice the flesh. There's no need to peel the squash; the skin becomes soft and tender once cooked.

With so many good green salsas now available in the supermarket, it's easy to recreate this Mexican restaurant favorite at home. For convenience, substitute shredded meat from a rotisserie chicken for the poached chicken.

TOSTADAS SALSA VERDE

SERVES 4 ■ PREP TIME: 20 MINUTES ■ TOTAL TIME: 30 MINUTES

4 flour tortillas (6-inch)
3 ounces (¾ cup) shredded pepper Jack cheese
2½ cups (10 ounces) shredded poached chicken (page 350)
1 cup jarred green salsa, plus more for serving (optional)
¼ cup plus 2 tablespoons chopped cilantro
¼ teaspoon ground cumin
1 cup shredded iceberg lettuce
3 plum tomatoes, diced
¼ cup sour cream

1 Preheat the oven to 400°F. Arrange the tortillas on a rimmed baking sheet. Sprinkle the cheese evenly over the tortillas; bake until golden brown, 8 to 10 minutes.

2 Meanwhile, in a medium bowl, toss together the chicken, salsa, the ¼ cup cilantro, and the cumin. Spoon the mixture evenly over the tortillas; bake until heated through, about 8 minutes.

3 Top with the lettuce, tomato, and sour cream. Sprinkle with the remaining cilantro. Serve immediately, with additional green salsa, if desired.

When cutting the beef into strips, slice against the grain (across the striated fibers); the result will be meat that is much more tender.

BEEF AND ORANGE STIR-FRY

SERVES 4 ■ PREP TIME: 25 MINUTES ■ **TOTAL TIME: 25 MINUTES**

3 oranges

2 garlic cloves, minced

2 tablespoons soy sauce

1½ pounds trimmed boneless sirloin or rib-eye steak, cut into ½-inch-thick strips

1 tablespoon cornstarch

1 to 2 tablespoons canola oil

6 scallions, green parts only, cut into 1-inch lengths

White rice, for serving

1 Into a small bowl, finely grate the zest and squeeze the juice from 1 orange. Add the garlic and soy sauce.

2 With a sharp paring knife, peel the remaining 2 oranges. Slice the oranges crosswise ½ inch thick, then halve the slices; push out and discard any seeds. Set aside.

3 In a medium bowl, toss the meat with the cornstarch until coated. Heat 1 tablespoon oil in a large nonstick skillet over high heat. Working in batches (adding more oil if needed), brown the beef on all sides, 3 to 5 minutes; transfer to a plate.

4 Pour the juice mixture into the skillet, and boil until syrupy, about 1 minute. Return the beef to the skillet; add the orange slices and scallions. Toss until coated and heated through. Serve hot, with white rice.

PREP TIME | **25** MINUTES

This Korean dish is usually eaten wrapped in lettuce leaves, but you could serve it over white rice instead. For added spice, serve Asian chile-garlic sauce on the side.

BEEF BULGOGI

SERVES 4 ■ PREP TIME: 20 MINUTES ■ **TOTAL TIME: 45 MINUTES**

1½ pounds rib-eye steak, trimmed of excess fat

¼ cup soy sauce

1 tablespoon hot chile sesame oil (see note below)

2 tablespoons dark brown sugar

6 garlic cloves, minced

1 tablespoon finely grated peeled fresh ginger

2 medium red onions, halved and cut lengthwise into 1-inch wedges

1 green bell pepper, seeds and ribs removed, sliced into ½-inch strips

4 teaspoons vegetable oil

1 small head Boston lettuce, separated into leaves

1 Freeze the beef for 20 minutes; transfer to a clean work surface. Slice diagonally (across the grain) into ⅛-inch-thick strips. In a small bowl, whisk together the soy sauce, sesame oil, brown sugar, garlic, and ginger. Place the onions and peppers in a small bowl; toss with half the soy marinade. Toss the steak in the remaining marinade; let stand for 15 minutes.

2 Heat 2 teaspoons of the vegetable oil in a large nonstick skillet over medium-high heat. Add the onions and peppers; cook until softened, about 5 minutes. Transfer to a plate. Wipe the skillet clean with a paper towel.

3 Heat the remaining 2 teaspoons vegetable oil over high heat. Cook half the meat, turning often, until browned, about 2 minutes. Transfer to a plate. Cook the remaining meat. Return the first batch and any accumulated juices to the pan; add the onion mixture. Cook, tossing, until heated through, about 1 minute. To serve, roll up the beef mixture in lettuce leaves.

NOTE
If you can't find hot chile sesame oil, add a dash of red pepper flakes to 1 tablespoon toasted sesame oil.

Soft hamburger buns work best with these kid-friendly sandwiches. Serve with pickles or potato chips.

SLOPPY JOES

SERVES 4 ■ PREP TIME: 20 MINUTES ■ **TOTAL TIME: 40 MINUTES**

1 tablespoon canola oil

1 medium onion, finely chopped

½ green bell pepper, ribs and seeds removed, finely chopped

1 celery stalk, finely chopped

2 garlic cloves, minced

Coarse salt and fresh ground pepper

1 pound ground beef

1 can (15 ounces) tomato sauce

¼ cup ketchup

1 tablespoon Worcestershire sauce

4 hamburger buns, split and toasted

1 In a large skillet, heat the oil over medium-high heat. Add the onion, bell pepper, celery, and garlic; season with salt and pepper. Cook, stirring frequently, until the vegetables are softened, 5 to 7 minutes.

2 Add the ground beef to the skillet. Cook, breaking up the meat with a wooden spoon, until it is no longer pink, 6 to 8 minutes.

3 Stir the tomato sauce, ketchup, and Worcestershire sauce into the beef mixture in the skillet. Simmer until thickened, stirring occasionally, 6 to 8 minutes.

4 Season the mixture with more salt and pepper, as desired. Spoon onto the buns, and serve immediately.

PLANNING AHEAD
Sloppy Joe mixture keeps in the freezer for up to 3 months. Freeze individual portions, then defrost as needed.

Serving a sandwich for dinner can make even the busiest day feel less complicated. Start with a mixed-green salad, and try Parmesan Steak Fries (page 83) on the side.

STEAK AND ONION SANDWICHES

SERVES 4 ■ PREP TIME: 20 MINUTES ■ **TOTAL TIME: 20 MINUTES**

3 tablespoons olive oil

2 medium onions, sliced into ½-inch-thick rings

Coarse salt and fresh ground pepper

4 minute steaks (3 ounces each)

2 tablespoons Worcestershire sauce

Toasted country bread

1 Heat 2 tablespoons of the olive oil in a large skillet over medium-high heat; cook the onions until browned, tossing occasionally, 10 to 15 minutes. Season with salt and pepper; remove.

2 Heat the remaining tablespoon of olive oil in the same skillet over high heat. Season the steaks with salt and pepper. Cook for 30 seconds on each side; remove. Add the Worcestershire sauce and 2 tablespoons water to the skillet, scraping up the browned bits with a wooden spoon. Return the onions to the skillet; toss.

3 Sandwich the steak and onions between toasted country bread. Serve immediately.

Caraway seeds often season cabbage dishes; here they give pork a tangy coating. If you plan to make the cabbage to serve on the side, begin preparing that recipe first, since the total time is about an hour.

RYE-CRUSTED PORK MEDALLIONS

SERVES 4 ■ PREP TIME: 25 MINUTES ■ **TOTAL TIME: 25 MINUTES**

3 to 4 slices rye bread with caraway seeds

Coarse salt and fresh ground pepper

1 large egg

1½ pounds boneless center-cut pork loin, sliced into 8 medallions (each ½ inch thick)

2 tablespoons canola oil

Grainy mustard, for serving (optional)

1 In a food processor, pulse enough of the bread to measure 2 cups of coarse crumbs. Transfer to a large bowl; season with salt and pepper. In another large bowl, whisk the egg with 1 teaspoon water.

2 Season the pork on both sides with salt and pepper. Dip each medallion in the egg mixture with one hand, then use the other hand to dredge in the breadcrumbs. Transfer to a plate.

3 Heat 1 tablespoon of the oil in a large nonstick skillet over medium heat. Place half the medallions in the skillet; cook until the pork is golden brown and the center is no longer pink, 3 to 4 minutes per side. Transfer to a plate; wipe the skillet clean. Repeat with the remaining medallions in the remaining oil. Serve with the mustard on the side, if desired.

RED CABBAGE WITH APPLE

2 slices bacon, cut into ½-inch strips

1 small onion, halved and thinly sliced

1 small head red cabbage, cored, quartered, and thinly sliced

1 green apple, peeled and thinly sliced

3 tablespoons cider vinegar

Coarse salt and fresh ground pepper

1 In a Dutch oven over medium heat, cook the bacon until browned, 10 minutes. Add the onion; cook until soft, 5 minutes.

2 Add the cabbage, apple, vinegar, and ¼ cup water. Cook, stirring, until the cabbage wilts, 5 minutes. Season with salt and pepper.

3 Cover; cook, stirring occasionally, over medium-low heat to desired softness (if the mixture is sticking, add water), 45 minutes to 1 hour. **SERVES 4**

PREP TIME | **15** MINUTES

If your broiler is located inside the oven (rather than in a separate compartment underneath), place the pork on the top shelf and the pineapple on the shelf below.

GLAZED PORK TENDERLOIN WITH PINEAPPLE

SERVES 4 ■ PREP TIME: 15 MINUTES ■ **TOTAL TIME: 45 MINUTES**

4 slices (each ½ inch thick) fresh pineapple

3 tablespoons dark hoisin sauce

2 teaspoons grated peeled fresh ginger

1 garlic clove, minced

1 teaspoon Dijon mustard

1½ pounds pork tenderloin, trimmed
Coarse salt and fresh ground pepper
Quick Ginger Sauce (recipe below), for serving

1 Heat the broiler. Place the pineapple slices on a foil-lined baking sheet.

2 In a small bowl, combine the hoisin sauce, ginger, garlic, and mustard.

3 Place the pork on a broiler pan fitted with a rack. Brush with the hoisin mixture; season with salt and pepper.

4 Place the pork in the broiler, about 4 inches from the heat; place the pineapple in the oven. Broil the pork until it registers 155°F on an instant-read thermometer, 15 to 20 minutes. Remove from the broiler (let rest at least 10 minutes before slicing; the temperature will rise to 160°F as the pork sits). Turn the pineapple slices; cook until browned in spots, about 10 minutes more.

5 Halve the pineapple slices; arrange on a platter with the sliced pork. Drizzle the pork with the pan juices; season with salt and pepper. Serve with the quick ginger sauce.

QUICK GINGER SAUCE

2 tablespoons dark hoisin sauce

2 tablespoons pineapple juice

2 teaspoons grated peeled fresh ginger

1 teaspoon soy sauce
Fresh ground pepper

In a small bowl, stir together the hoisin sauce, pineapple juice, ginger, and soy sauce; season with pepper.

If you prefer, you can replace the white wine with an equal amount of apple cider. To prevent peeled apples from turning brown, place them in a bowl of cold water mixed with the juice of one lemon.

PORK CHOPS WITH APPLES AND SHALLOTS

SERVES 4 ■ PREP TIME: 30 MINUTES ■ TOTAL TIME: 45 MINUTES

2 tablespoons butter
½ pound medium shallots, halved or quartered lengthwise (pieces should be about ¾ inch thick)
2 Granny Smith apples, peeled, cored, and cut into eighths
½ cup white wine
4 pork rib chops (each ½ inch thick and 6 to 8 ounces)
 Coarse salt and fresh ground pepper

1 Heat the broiler; set a rack 4 inches from the heat. In a large skillet, heat the butter over medium-high heat. Add the shallots; cook, stirring occasionally, until browned, about 5 minutes. Cover the pan; reduce the heat to medium. Continue cooking until the shallots are soft, about 5 minutes more.

2 Add the apples and wine; cover, and cook until the apples are beginning to soften, about 5 minutes. Uncover; cook, stirring, until most of the liquid has evaporated and the apples are tender, 2 to 4 minutes more. Remove from the heat; cover to keep warm.

3 While the apples are cooking, season the pork chops generously with salt and pepper; place on a rimmed baking sheet. Broil until cooked through, 3 to 5 minutes per side. To serve, spoon the warm apple mixture over the chops.

WILTED SPINACH WITH NUTMEG

2 tablespoons butter
2 packages (10 ounces each) fresh spinach, rinsed, tough ends discarded
 Pinch of ground nutmeg
 Coarse salt and fresh ground pepper

In a large, deep saucepan with a tight-fitting lid, melt the butter over medium heat. Add the spinach (with water still clinging to the leaves); cover, and cook until wilted, stirring halfway through, about 5 minutes. Remove from the heat. Season with the nutmeg, salt, and pepper. Serve immediately, with a slotted spoon.
SERVES 4

PREP TIME | **30** MINUTES

Lamb topped with yogurt sauce is a staple of Middle Eastern cooking. In this recipe, the yogurt is flavored with shallots, cilantro, and lemon juice.

LAMB CHOPS WITH YOGURT SAUCE

SERVES 4 ■ PREP TIME: 20 MINUTES ■ **TOTAL TIME: 20 MINUTES**

4 lamb rib or shoulder chops (about 8 ounces each)

Coarse salt and fresh ground pepper

2 tablespoons olive oil

½ cup plain low-fat yogurt

1 tablespoon minced shallot

2 teaspoons chopped fresh cilantro

2 teaspoons fresh lemon juice

1 Season both sides of the lamb chops generously with salt and pepper. Heat the oil in a large skillet over medium-high heat. Cook the lamb (in two batches, if necessary) until an instant-read thermometer inserted into the thickest part registers 140°F for medium-rare, 4 to 6 minutes per side. Let rest, covered, for 10 minutes.

2 Meanwhile, make the sauce: In a medium bowl, whisk together the yogurt, shallot, cilantro, and lemon juice; season with salt and pepper. Serve with the lamb.

ORZO AND SNAP PEA SALAD

Coarse salt and fresh ground pepper

½ pound orzo

1 pound sugar snap peas, trimmed and halved crosswise

2 small yellow squash, halved lengthwise and cut crosswise into ½-inch pieces

3 tablespoons fresh lemon juice

2 tablespoons olive oil

2 tablespoons finely grated Parmesan cheese

1 In a large pot of boiling salted water, cook the orzo for 5 minutes. Add the peas and squash. Cook until the orzo is al dente and the vegetables are crisp-tender, about 3 minutes. Drain well; return to the pot.

2 Add the lemon juice, olive oil, and cheese. Season generously with salt and pepper. Toss to combine. SERVES 4

The cooking time for lentils can vary widely depending on their age, as older lentils require more time. For the best results, buy a fresh, new bag. A mustard vinaigrette boosts the flavor of this Mediterranean-inspired dish.

ROASTED SALMON WITH LENTILS

SERVES 4 ■ PREP TIME: 10 MINUTES ■ **TOTAL TIME: 45 MINUTES**

¾ cup lentils, picked over
 and rinsed
½ small onion, chopped
1 large celery stalk, chopped
2 tablespoons red-wine vinegar
1 tablespoon olive oil
1 tablespoon Dijon mustard
1 garlic clove, minced
⅓ cup chopped fresh parsley
 Coarse salt and
 fresh ground pepper
4 skinless salmon fillets
 (6 ounces each)
 Nonstick cooking spray

1 Combine the lentils and 2½ cups water in a medium saucepan. Bring to a boil; reduce the heat, and simmer, covered, for 5 minutes. Add the onion and celery; cover, and continue cooking until the lentils and vegetables are just tender, 15 to 25 minutes more. Drain, reserving the cooking liquid. Transfer the lentil mixture to a medium bowl.

2 In a bowl, whisk 2 tablespoons of the reserved cooking liquid with the vinegar, oil, mustard, garlic, and parsley; season with salt and pepper. Toss half the dressing with the lentil mixture.

3 Heat the broiler. Season the salmon with salt and pepper. Coat a baking sheet with cooking spray. Arrange the salmon on the sheet; broil until opaque throughout, 8 to 10 minutes. Spoon the lentils onto 4 plates; top with the salmon, flaking it into large pieces, if desired. Drizzle with the remaining dressing.

USING CELERY LEAVES
Chopped celery leaves add wonderful flavor to the lentils. Use them in place of or in addition to the parsley.

Here's our do-it-yourself take on the popular restaurant sandwich originally from New Orleans. Almost any type of coleslaw (see recipes on pages 35, 83, 171, and 232) would work as an accompaniment.

FISH PO'BOYS

SERVES 4 ■ PREP TIME: 30 MINUTES ■ **TOTAL TIME: 30 MINUTES**

1 pound skinless flounder fillets

2 tablespoons yellow cornmeal

Coarse salt and fresh ground pepper

2 tablespoons canola oil

8-ounce baguette, split and hollowed out slightly

Spicy Tartar Sauce (recipe below)

Lettuce, for serving

Sliced tomato, for serving

1 Cut the flounder fillets into 1½-inch strips; pat dry. Place in a medium bowl. Add the cornmeal; season with salt and pepper. Toss to coat.

2 Heat the canola oil in a large nonstick skillet over high heat. Brown the fish (work in batches if needed) on both sides, 7 to 10 minutes (turn the fish carefully). Transfer to a paper-towel lined plate; season with more salt, as desired.

3 Spread both halves of the baguette with tartar sauce, and layer with lettuce, tomato, and fish. Cut into 4 portions and serve.

SPICY TARTAR SAUCE

½ cup reduced-fat mayonnaise

2 tablespoons chili sauce

2 tablespoons chopped fresh parsley

2 tablespoons grainy mustard

2 tablespoons chopped gherkins (or pickles)

Hot sauce, such as Tabasco

In a small bowl, combine the mayonnaise, chili sauce, parsley, mustard, and gherkins. Season with hot sauce, as desired. The sauce can be refrigerated, covered, for 2 to 3 days.

The three main ingredients in this recipe—pecans, cornmeal, and catfish—are all common in Southern cooking. The carrot slaw served on the side is lighter in fat and calories than more traditional mayonnaise-based slaws.

PECAN-CRUSTED CATFISH

SERVES 4 ■ PREP TIME: 10 MINUTES ■ TOTAL TIME: 30 MINUTES

⅓ cup yellow cornmeal
¼ cup pecans
  Coarse salt and
  fresh ground pepper
4 skinless catfish fillets
  (6 ounces each),
  rinsed and patted dry
4 tablespoons vegetable oil
  Lemon wedges (optional)

1 Grind the cornmeal and pecans with 1 teaspoon salt and ¼ teaspoon pepper in a food processor until the nuts are finely ground. Transfer to a large, shallow container. Dredge the catfish in the cornmeal mixture, patting it on to coat completely.

2 Heat 2 tablespoons of the oil in a large nonstick skillet over medium-high heat. Cook 2 fish fillets until golden brown and firm to the touch, 4 to 5 minutes per side. Transfer the fish to a plate; sprinkle with salt, and cover to keep warm.

3 Wipe the skillet with a paper towel. Repeat with the remaining 2 tablespoons oil and fish. Serve with lemon wedges, if desired.

CARROT SLAW WITH YOGURT DRESSING

1 pound carrots, peeled
½ cup plain low-fat yogurt
2 tablespoons cider vinegar
1 tablespoon Dijon mustard
¼ teaspoon sugar
¼ cup finely chopped red onion
  Coarse salt and
  fresh ground pepper
½ small white cabbage,
  halved crosswise and thinly
  sliced (5 cups)
2 tablespoons chopped fresh dill

In a food processor fitted with the shredding disk (or on the large holes of a box grater), grate the carrots. In a large bowl, whisk together the yogurt, vinegar, mustard, sugar, and onion; season with salt and pepper. Add the carrots, cabbage, and dill to the bowl; toss well. Top the mixture with a plate that fits inside the bowl; weight with a heavy object. Let sit at room temperature for 20 minutes before serving. **SERVES 6**

Quinoa adds protein as well as a chewy texture to this meatless main dish. The heat of the cooked quinoa and mushrooms helps wilt the spinach; the dressing and feta pull this warm salad together.

WARM QUINOA, SPINACH, AND SHIITAKE SALAD

SERVES 4 ■ PREP TIME: 30 MINUTES **■ TOTAL TIME: 40 MINUTES**

½ cup red-wine vinegar

⅔ cup olive oil

Coarse salt and fresh ground pepper

2 pounds fresh shiitake mushrooms, stems removed, caps halved

1½ cups quinoa

1 pound baby spinach

1½ cups crumbled feta cheese (8 ounces)

1 Heat the broiler; set a rack 4 inches from the heat. In a small bowl, whisk together the vinegar, oil, 1 teaspoon salt, and ¼ teaspoon pepper.

2 On a large rimmed broiler-proof baking sheet, toss the mushrooms with half the dressing (reserve the rest); broil, tossing occasionally, until most of the liquid has evaporated and the mushrooms are tender, 20 to 25 minutes.

3 Meanwhile, in a small saucepan, combine the quinoa, 3 cups water, and 1½ teaspoons salt. Bring to a boil; reduce the heat to medium. Cover, and simmer until the liquid has been absorbed, 15 to 20 minutes.

4 Place the spinach in a large bowl; add the hot mushrooms, quinoa, and reserved dressing. Toss to combine (the spinach will wilt slightly). Top with the crumbled feta, and serve immediately.

CLEANING SHIITAKES
Do not soak shiitakes in water, because they will become spongy. Instead, wipe the caps clean with a damp paper towel after trimming away the stems.

Serve this brightly colored, layered tortilla pie with salsa and sour cream on the side. You can assemble the dish ahead of time, then bake it just before serving.

TORTILLA AND BLACK BEAN PIE

SERVES 6 ■ PREP TIME: 25 MINUTES ■ **TOTAL TIME: 1 HOUR**

4 flour tortillas (10-inch)
1 tablespoon canola oil
1 large onion, diced
1 jalapeño chile, minced (remove seeds and ribs for less heat)
2 garlic cloves, minced
½ teaspoon ground cumin
   Coarse salt and fresh ground pepper
2 cans (15 ounces each) black beans, drained and rinsed
12 ounces beer, or 1½ cups water
1 package (10 ounces) frozen corn
4 scallions, thinly sliced, plus more for garnish
2½ cups shredded Cheddar cheese (8 ounces)

1 Preheat the oven to 400°F. Using a paring knife, trim the tortillas to fit a 9-inch springform pan, using the bottom of the pan as a guide. Set aside.

2 Heat the oil in a skillet over medium heat. Add the onion, jalapeño, garlic, and cumin; season with salt and pepper. Cook, stirring occasionally, until the onion is softened, 5 to 7 minutes.

3 Add the beans and beer to the skillet, and bring to a boil. Reduce the heat to medium; simmer until the liquid has almost evaporated, 8 to 10 minutes. Stir in the corn and scallions, and remove from the heat. Season with salt and pepper.

4 Fit a trimmed tortilla in the bottom of the springform pan; layer with one quarter of the beans and ½ cup cheese. Repeat three times, using 1 cup cheese on the top layer. Bake until hot and the cheese is melted, 20 to 25 minutes. Unmold the pie; sprinkle with scallions. Slice into wedges, and serve immediately.

PREP TIME | **20** MINUTES

Freshly roasted peppers impart a smoky taste to this hearty pasta. If you like, you can use jarred peppers, thinly sliced, instead of making your own, and skip step one.

ORECCHIETTE WITH SAUSAGE AND ROASTED PEPPERS

SERVES 6 ■ PREP TIME: 20 MINUTES ■ TOTAL TIME: 40 MINUTES

2 medium red bell peppers, four flat sides sliced off core, ribs and seeds discarded

2 medium yellow bell peppers, four flat sides sliced off core, ribs and seeds discarded

Coarse salt and fresh ground pepper

1 pound orecchiette or other short pasta

2 teaspoons olive oil

1 pound sweet Italian sausage, removed from casings

1 tablespoon butter, cut into small pieces

⅓ cup grated Parmesan cheese

1 Heat the broiler. Place the peppers, skin side up, on a foil-lined baking sheet; broil 4 inches from the heat until charred, 18 to 20 minutes. Transfer to a large bowl. Cover with plastic wrap; steam for 2 to 3 minutes. Using a paper towel, rub off the pepper skins, reserving any juices in the bowl. Thinly slice the peppers crosswise into ¼-inch strips; return to the bowl. Set aside.

2 In a large pot of boiling salted water, cook the pasta until al dente according to the package instructions. Drain, reserving ½ cup of the pasta water.

3 Meanwhile, heat the oil in a large skillet over medium heat. Cook the sausage, breaking it up with a spoon, until browned, 7 to 10 minutes. Add the roasted peppers; cook until heated through.

4 Transfer the sausage mixture to a large bowl; add the pasta, butter, reserved pasta water, and Parmesan. Season with salt and pepper. Toss to combine.

Whole-wheat pasta, which contains more fiber and is slightly chewier and nuttier tasting than regular pasta, adds nutritional value to this dish.

WHOLE-WHEAT PASTA WITH ROASTED EGGPLANT AND TOMATOES

SERVES 6 ■ PREP TIME: 15 MINUTES ■ **TOTAL TIME: 45 MINUTES**

1½ pounds eggplant, peeled in alternating stripes and cut into ¾-inch pieces

1 large onion, halved and cut into ½-inch wedges

2 pints (4 cups) cherry tomatoes Coarse salt and fresh ground pepper

¼ cup olive oil

¾ pound whole-wheat penne (or other short, tubular pasta)

¼ cup sliced pitted kalamata or oil-cured black olives

½ cup finely grated Parmesan cheese, plus more for serving

1 Preheat the oven to 450°F. In a medium (11-by-15-inch) roasting pan, combine the eggplant, onion, tomatoes, 1½ teaspoons salt, ¼ teaspoon pepper, and oil; toss well to coat. Roast until tender, tossing mixture halfway through, about 30 minutes.

2 Meanwhile, cook the pasta in a large pot of boiling salted water until al dente according to the package instructions. Reserve ½ cup of the pasta water; drain the pasta, and return it to the pot.

3 Add the roasted eggplant mixture, olives, and Parmesan. Toss to coat, adding ¼ to ½ cup of the reserved pasta water, if desired. Serve immediately, sprinkled with more cheese.

PREP TIME | **15** MINUTES

Here is a meaty tomato sauce that doesn't need to cook for a long time to be flavorful. And the sauce keeps well in the freezer for up to 3 months.

PASTA AND EASY ITALIAN MEAT SAUCE

SERVES 6 ■ PREP TIME: 15 MINUTES ■ **TOTAL TIME: 30 MINUTES**

4 tablespoons butter
1 tablespoon olive oil
1 carrot, grated (about ½ cup)
1 onion, chopped
2 garlic cloves, chopped
¾ pound ground beef
1 can (28 ounces) whole tomatoes
½ cup milk
1 dried bay leaf
½ teaspoon dried thyme
¼ teaspoon ground nutmeg
  Coarse salt and
  fresh ground pepper
1 pound fettuccine
  Grated Parmesan cheese,
  for serving

1 Heat the butter and oil in a large saucepan over medium heat. Stir in the carrot, onion, and garlic. Add the ground beef, and cook until it turns from pink to brown, about 5 minutes.

2 Add the tomatoes and their liquid, crushing them with the back of a large spoon. Stir in the milk, bay leaf, thyme, nutmeg, ½ teaspoon salt, and ⅛ teaspoon pepper. Simmer for 20 minutes.

3 Meanwhile, in a large pot of boiling salted water, cook the fettuccine until al dente according to the package instructions. Reserve about ½ cup of the cooking water, and drain the fettuccine. Return it to the warm pot. Add the meat sauce, and toss. Add the reserved pasta water as needed if the sauce seems dry. To serve, sprinkle with Parmesan.

REGIONAL RAGÙ
Our sauce is based on the famed Ragù alla Bolognese (sauce in the style of Bologna). The addition of milk might seem to be unusual, but it's traditional in northern Italy—where butter and cream, as well as milk, are essential to the cuisine.

In this foolproof pasta dish, the cherry tomatoes cook just long enough to bring out their juice, which blends with the garlic-flavored olive oil to make a great-tasting sauce.

TOMATO AND OLIVE PENNE

SERVES 4 ■ PREP TIME: 15 MINUTES ■ **TOTAL TIME: 25 MINUTES**

Coarse salt and
fresh ground pepper

1 pound penne or other short pasta

¼ cup olive oil

2 garlic cloves, thinly sliced

¼ pound cherry tomatoes (2 cups), halved or quartered

1 teaspoon dried oregano

¼ teaspoon red pepper flakes (optional)

¼ cup kalamata olives, pitted and sliced

¼ cup chopped fresh parsley

¼ cup grated Parmesan cheese, plus more for serving (optional)

1 In a large pot of boiling salted water, cook the penne until al dente according to the package instructions. Drain.

2 Meanwhile, in a large skillet, heat the olive oil over medium heat. Add the garlic, and cook, stirring, until just golden, about 1 minute. Add the cherry tomatoes, oregano, red pepper flakes, ½ teaspoon salt, and ¼ teaspoon pepper. Reduce the heat to low, and cook, stirring, until the tomato juices run, about 3 minutes.

3 Add the penne, olives, parsley, and ¼ cup Parmesan to the skillet and toss to combine. Serve with more cheese, if desired.

PITTING OLIVES
The easiest way to pit an olive is to lay a wide chef's knife over it and smack the blade with your fist or the palm of your hand. The olive should split open, and the pit will pop right out.

ROASTED ACORN SQUASH, SHALLOTS, AND ROSEMARY

- 2 acorn squash (2 pounds each), halved
- 8 shallots, peeled, root ends left intact (separate into lobes, if large)
- 6 small sprigs fresh rosemary
- 3 tablespoons olive oil
- ¼ cup balsamic vinegar
  Coarse salt and fresh ground pepper

1 Preheat the oven to 450°F. Carefully cut each squash half into four wedges.

2 Combine the squash on a rimmed baking sheet with the shallots, rosemary, olive oil, and vinegar. Season with 2 teaspoons salt and ½ teaspoon pepper; toss well to coat, and spread in a single layer.

3 Roast, turning the squash halfway through, until browned and tender, 35 to 40 minutes. **SERVES 4**

BUTTERMILK MASHED POTATOES

- 1½ pounds (4 medium) new potatoes, peeled and cut into 1-inch pieces
  Coarse salt and fresh ground pepper
- ¼ to ½ cup buttermilk
- 2 tablespoons butter, cut into small pieces

1 Place the potatoes in a large saucepan; add enough cold water to cover by 2 inches. Bring to a boil; add 1 tablespoon salt, and cook until the potatoes are very tender when pierced with the tip of a paring knife, 20 to 25 minutes.

2 Drain; place in a large bowl. Mash with a potato masher, then add the buttermilk and butter. Season with salt and pepper. Mash until smooth and combined. **SERVES 4**

BRUSSELS SPROUTS AND HAZELNUTS

- Coarse salt and fresh ground pepper
- 1 pound Brussels sprouts, trimmed and scored
- 1 tablespoon butter
- 2 tablespoons chopped blanched hazelnuts

1 In a large skillet over medium heat, bring 1 cup water and ½ teaspoon salt to a boil. Add the Brussels sprouts; reduce the heat to a simmer. Cover; cook, stirring occasionally, until tender, about 20 minutes (add more water if the pan becomes dry).

2 Uncover; raise the heat to medium-high, and cook until the water has evaporated. Add the butter and hazelnuts; cook until the nuts are fragrant, 3 to 5 minutes. Season with salt and pepper. **SERVES 4**

ROASTED FENNEL

- 2 medium fennel bulbs (8 ounces each)
- 1 tablespoon olive oil
  Coarse salt and fresh ground pepper

1 Preheat the oven to 425°F. Trim the fennel bulbs. Halve the bulbs lengthwise; slice lengthwise into ½-inch-thick pieces.

2 On a rimmed baking sheet, toss the fennel with the olive oil; season with salt and pepper. Roast, turning once, until browned, 25 to 30 minutes. **SERVES 4**

SAUTÉED BOK CHOY AND BROCCOLI

 1 pound bok choy
 1 pound broccoli
 2 tablespoons canola oil
 1 garlic clove, chopped
 1 tablespoon finely grated peeled fresh ginger
 1 to 2 tablespoons soy sauce

1 Cut the white stalks from the bok choy; slice the stems into 1-inch pieces. Coarsely chop the green leaves. Peel the stalks from the broccoli; slice ¼ inch thick. Cut the florets into bite-size pieces.

2 In a large skillet, boil ½ cup water. Add the bok choy stalks and broccoli; cover. Simmer over medium-low heat until the broccoli is bright green, 5 to 7 minutes. Uncover; cook on high heat until the water evaporates, 2 to 4 minutes. Add the bok choy leaves, oil, and garlic. Cook, tossing often, until the garlic is fragrant, 2 minutes.

3 Press the ginger in a sieve over the skillet to release its juices. Stir in the soy sauce. **SERVES 4**

SAUTÉED MUSHROOMS WITH THYME

 2 tablespoons butter
 1 tablespoon olive oil
 1 small shallot, minced
 1½ pounds small white mushrooms, halved
     Coarse salt and fresh ground pepper
 1 teaspoon minced fresh thyme
 ¼ cup dry red or white wine (or water)

1 In a skillet over medium-low heat, melt the butter with the oil. Add the shallot; cook, stirring, until soft, about 5 minutes. Raise the heat to medium. Add the mushrooms; season with salt and pepper. Cook, covered, until the mushrooms release their liquid, 5 to 6 minutes.

2 Uncover; raise the heat to high. Cook, tossing, until the liquid evaporates and the mushrooms are brown, 3 to 5 minutes. Add the thyme and wine (or water). Cook until the skillet is almost dry, 1 minute. Serve hot. **SERVES 4**

SWISS CHARD WITH TOASTED BREADCRUMBS

 2½ tablespoons butter
 ½ cup fresh breadcrumbs
     Coarse salt and fresh ground pepper
 2 pounds Swiss chard
     Sugar (optional)

1 In a 5-quart saucepan, melt ½ tablespoon of the butter over medium heat. Add the breadcrumbs and a pinch each of salt and pepper. Cook, tossing, until golden brown, 2 to 3 minutes. Set aside; wipe the pan with a paper towel.

2 Trim the chard; slice crosswise ¾ inch thick, keeping the stems separate from the greens. In the pan, melt the remaining 2 tablespoons butter over medium-high. Cook the stems, stirring, until tender, 4 to 6 minutes. Add the greens; cover and cook over medium-low until wilted, 5 minutes. Uncover; cook, stirring, over medium-high until the pan is dry, 6 to 8 minutes.

3 Season with salt and pepper; add a pinch of sugar, if desired. Top with the toasted breadcrumbs. **SERVES 4**

ROASTED PEARS AND SWEET POTATOES

 2 sweet potatoes
 3 tablespoons olive oil
 1 teaspoon dry mustard
 ½ teaspoon ground ginger
 ¼ teaspoon cayenne pepper
     Coarse salt
 2 Bartlett pears

1 Preheat the oven to 400°F. Scrub the sweet potatoes. Quarter lengthwise; slice diagonally 1½ inches thick. On a rimmed baking sheet, toss the slices with 2 tablespoons of the olive oil, the mustard, ginger, and cayenne; season with coarse salt. Roast, tossing occasionally, until crisp-tender, 20 to 25 minutes.

2 Core and quarter the pears; halve crosswise. Add to the potatoes; toss all with the remaining tablespoon oil. Continue roasting until the potatoes are fork-tender, about 10 minutes more. **SERVES 4**

This dessert is more interesting when prepared with a variety of stone fruits, but if you can't find one particular type, substitute more of another. You could also use apricots in place of any of the other three fruits.

ROASTED FRUIT

SERVES 4 ■ PREP TIME: 10 MINUTES ■ **TOTAL TIME: 30 MINUTES**

2 peaches
2 plums
2 nectarines
2 sprigs fresh rosemary
2 to 3 tablespoons sugar (depending on sweetness of fruit)
2 tablespoons unsalted butter, cut into pieces
1 tablespoon fresh lime juice
  Vanilla ice cream or frozen yogurt (optional)

1 Preheat the oven to 400°F. With a fork, prick the skins of the peaches, plums, and nectarines. Halve each fruit, and remove the pits. Halve the fruit again.

2 In a roasting pan, toss the fruit with the rosemary, sugar, butter, and lime juice. Roast, tossing occasionally, until the fruit is fork-tender, 15 to 20 minutes.

3 Serve warm over vanilla ice cream or frozen yogurt, if desired, and drizzle the pan juices over the top.

We like Granny Smith apples for this tart, but you could substitute a number of other varieties, including Macoun, Cortland, or Jonagold.

RUSTIC APPLE TART

SERVES 4 TO 6 ■ PREP TIME: 20 MINUTES ■ **TOTAL TIME: 1 HOUR**

Flour, for work surface
1 sheet frozen puff pastry (from a 17.3-ounce package), thawed but not unfolded
3 Granny Smith apples
⅓ cup sugar
1 large egg yolk beaten with 1 teaspoon water, for egg wash
2 tablespoons unsalted butter
2 tablespoons apple jelly or apricot jam

1 Preheat the oven to 375°F. On a lightly floured work surface, roll out the pastry sheet (still folded) to an 8-by-14-inch rectangle. Trim the edges with a sharp paring knife. Transfer to a baking sheet; place in the freezer. Peel, core, and slice the apples ¼ inch thick. Toss in a large bowl with the sugar.

2 Brush the pastry with the egg wash, avoiding the edges. Use a sharp paring knife to score a ¾-inch border around the pastry (do not cut all the way through). Place the apples inside the border, and dot with the butter. Bake until the pastry is golden and the apples are tender, 30 to 35 minutes.

3 In the microwave or a small saucepan, heat the jelly with 1 tablespoon water until melted. Brush the apples with the glaze. Serve the tart warm or at room temperature, cutting into pieces with a serrated knife.

ROLLING OUT PUFF PASTRY
Store-bought frozen puff pastry sometimes cracks along seams when unfolded. To prevent this, leave the pastry folded when you roll it.

Here's a delightful take on the grilled sandwich. Because of the challah and the addition of eggs, butter, and milk, this dessert is richer than most, so it's best served after a light meal.

GRILLED CHOCOLATE SANDWICHES

SERVES 4 ■ PREP TIME: 15 MINUTES ■ **TOTAL TIME: 15 MINUTES**

2 large eggs

2 tablespoons milk

4 large slices challah or Italian bread (cut ¾ inch thick)

4 ounces thin semisweet chocolate bar

2 tablespoons unsalted butter

Confectioners' sugar, for dusting

1 In a large, shallow dish, whisk together the eggs and milk; set aside.

2 Form two sandwiches with the bread and chocolate (break the chocolate as necessary to cover the bread without extending over the edges); dip both sides of the sandwiches in the egg mixture to coat.

3 Heat the butter in a large skillet over medium heat; transfer the sandwiches to the skillet. Cook, pressing occasionally with a spatula, until golden, 1 to 2 minutes per side. Transfer to a paper-towel-lined plate. Cut each sandwich in half, and dust with confectioners' sugar before serving.

This crustless pie is an easy dessert to prepare from scratch. It's perfect for fall, when pears are at their peak. And because it has a custard base, it needs no accompaniment.

PEAR CUSTARD PIE

SERVES 6 ■ PREP TIME: 15 MINUTES ■ **TOTAL TIME: 1 HOUR**

¼ cup unsalted butter, melted, plus more for pie dish

3 ripe but firm Comice or Bartlett pears, peeled, halved, and cored

⅓ cup granulated sugar

⅓ cup all-purpose flour

2 teaspoons vanilla extract

3 large eggs

¾ cup milk

¼ teaspoon salt

Confectioners' sugar, for dusting

1 Preheat the oven to 350°F; butter a 9-inch pie dish. Slice the pears ¼ inch thick lengthwise. Arrange the slices, overlapping slightly, in the dish.

2 In a blender, process the melted butter, granulated sugar, flour, vanilla, eggs, milk, and salt until smooth.

3 Pour the batter over the pears; bake until golden and firm to the touch, 40 to 45 minutes. Serve warm or at room temperature, dusted with confectioners' sugar.

Amaretti are crunchy Italian macaroons made from almond paste, sugar, and egg whites. You can substitute any crispy cookie.

CAPPUCCINO PARFAITS

SERVES 4
PREP TIME: 10 MINUTES
TOTAL TIME: 40 MINUTES

- 1 container (15 ounces) part-skim ricotta
- ⅓ cup sugar
- 2 teaspoons instant espresso powder
- 4 crisp amaretti cookies

1 In a food processor, purée the ricotta, sugar, and espresso powder until very smooth, scraping down the sides of the bowl as needed, 1 to 2 minutes.

2 Dividing evenly, spoon the mixture into 4 glasses or serving dishes. Refrigerate, covered, until ready to serve, at least 30 minutes and up to 1 day.

3 Just before serving, crumble the cookies over the parfaits.

WINTER

WHEN THE AIR TURNS CHILLY, the pantry provides us with seasonings and ingredients to boost the flavor of everyday meals. We're cooking protein-rich meats, chicken, and fish, as well as winter squash, root vegetables, and potatoes—often with spices to liven everything up. And, as in every other season, the goal is to put fast, healthful, hassle-free meals on the table.

So, to offer a break from standard fare, this chapter includes delight-ful, pantry-based variations on the ever-popular chicken—you'll find it flavored with Moroccan spices and served over couscous; braised in a Mediterranean-inspired stew; shredded and tucked into enchiladas; and paired with prosciutto and sage in a classic Italian dish known as saltimbocca, or "jump in the mouth." Wintertime pastas feature rich, creamy sauces, including carbonara, a dish that requires just five ingre-dients but delivers comfort by the bowlful, and a baked macaroni and cheese tossed with ham and topped with savory breadcrumbs.

In-season desserts depend less on fresh fruits and more on deep, lus-cious ingredients like chocolate and ginger. We have molten choco-late mini cakes and a foolproof gingerbread with chocolate zigzagged through the batter, both homey treats to enjoy on a winter's night.

PREP TIME | **20** MINUTES

Like many other bean- and legume-based soups, this one is flavored with bacon. It can be served at the start of a Sunday dinner, or as a weeknight meal itself when paired with a green salad topped with Lemon-Parmesan Vinaigrette (page 347).

LENTIL SOUP

SERVES 4 ■ PREP TIME: 20 MINUTES ■ **TOTAL TIME: 1 HOUR**

3 strips bacon (3 ounces), cut into ½-inch pieces

1 large onion, chopped

3 medium carrots, peeled, halved lengthwise, and cut into ¼-inch half moons

3 garlic cloves, minced

2 tablespoons tomato paste

1½ cups lentils, picked over and rinsed

½ teaspoon dried thyme

2 cans (14.5 ounces each) reduced-sodium chicken broth (3½ cups)

1 tablespoon red-wine vinegar

Coarse salt and fresh ground pepper

1 In a Dutch oven (or other 5-quart pot with a tight-fitting lid), cook the bacon over medium-low heat until browned and crisp, 8 to 10 minutes. Pour off all but 1 tablespoon of the fat.

2 Add the onion and carrots; cook until softened, about 5 minutes. Stir in the garlic, and cook until fragrant, about 30 seconds. Stir in the tomato paste, and cook for 1 minute.

3 Add the lentils, thyme, broth, and 2 cups water. Bring to a boil; reduce to a simmer. Cover; cook until the lentils are tender, 30 to 45 minutes. If the soup becomes too thick during cooking, add up to 1 cup more water.

4 Stir in the vinegar, 1½ teaspoons salt, and ¼ teaspoon pepper. Serve the soup immediately.

When buying parsnips, choose those that are smooth, firm, and about 8 inches long, roughly the size of a large carrot. They should not be soft, spotted, or damp.

CREAMY PARSNIP SOUP

SERVES 4
PREP TIME: 20 MINUTES
TOTAL TIME: 50 MINUTES

- 2 tablespoons butter
- 1 pound (2 cups) prepared sliced leeks (see note, page 61)
- 1 pound parsnips, trimmed, peeled, and cut crosswise into 1-inch pieces
- 2 apples, peeled, cored, and cut into 1-inch pieces
- 1 medium baking potato (about ½ pound), peeled and cut into 1-inch pieces
- 1 can (14.5 ounces) reduced-sodium chicken broth
- ½ cup heavy cream
  Coarse salt and fresh ground pepper
  Leek Garnish (recipe opposite)

1 Heat the butter in a large pot over medium heat. Add the leeks (reserving ½ cup for garnish). Cook, stirring, for 5 minutes.

2 Add the parsnips, apples, potato, broth, and 4 cups water. Bring to a boil; reduce the heat and simmer, partially covered, until the vegetables are tender, 20 to 25 minutes.

3 Working in batches, purée the soup in a blender until smooth. Return it to the pot; stir in the cream. Season with salt and pepper. Top with the leek garnish.

LEEK GARNISH

1 tablespoon butter

½ cup prepared sliced
   leeks (see note,
   page 61)

In a large skillet, heat the butter over
medium-high heat. Add the leeks;
cook, stirring, until golden brown, about
3 minutes.

This sweet and spicy soup is wonderfully rich, even though it's made without a drop of cream. If your carrots don't taste sweet enough, add up to a teaspoon of sugar in step two.

CURRIED CARROT SOUP

SERVES 4 ■ PREP TIME: 20 MINUTES ■ **TOTAL TIME: 40 MINUTES**

2 tablespoons butter

1 cup chopped onion

1 teaspoon curry powder
   Coarse salt and
   fresh ground pepper

2 cans (14.5 ounces each)
   reduced-sodium chicken broth
   (about 3½ cups)

2 pounds carrots, peeled and
   cut into 1-inch chunks

1 to 2 tablespoons fresh
   lemon juice

2 tablespoons coarsely chopped
   fresh cilantro, for garnish
   (optional)

1 Heat the butter in a Dutch oven or large (4- to 5-quart) saucepan over medium heat. Add the onion, curry powder, 2 teaspoons salt, and ¼ teaspoon pepper. Cook, stirring occasionally, until the onion is soft, about 5 minutes.

2 Add the broth, carrots, and 3 cups water; bring to a boil. Reduce the heat; cover, and simmer until the carrots are tender, about 20 minutes.

3 In a blender, purée the soup in batches until smooth; hot liquids will expand when blended, so be careful not to fill the jar of the blender more than halfway. To prevent the liquid from spattering, allow the heat to escape: Remove the cap from the hole in the lid, and cover the lid with a dish towel when blending. Transfer to a clean saucepan. Add more water to thin to desired consistency. Reheat, if necessary. Stir in the lemon juice. Serve garnished with the cilantro, if desired.

CHILLING THE SOUP
This recipe can also be served chilled. Allow the soup to cool, then refrigerate in a covered container.

The salad dressing can be refrigerated in an airtight container for up to two weeks. Before serving, whisk the dressing to loosen.

ICEBERG WEDGES WITH THOUSAND ISLAND DRESSING

SERVES 4
PREP TIME: 10 MINUTES
TOTAL TIME: 10 MINUTES

- 1 cup reduced-fat mayonnaise
- ¼ cup tomato-based chili sauce
- ¼ cup milk
- 2 tablespoons red-wine vinegar
- 2 tablespoons sweet pickle relish
- 1 tablespoon chopped fresh parsley
- 1 scallion, thinly sliced
  Coarse salt and fresh ground pepper
- 1 head iceberg lettuce, cored and cut into 8 wedges

1 In a small bowl, whisk together the mayonnaise, chili sauce, milk, vinegar, relish, parsley, scallion, and ¼ teaspoon each salt and pepper.

2 Place the iceberg wedges on a platter or divide among 4 plates; drizzle with the dressing, as desired. Serve immediately.

The combination of fennel, citrus, and parsley makes this Italian-style salad an ideal palate cleanser. It tastes particularly refreshing in winter, when salad greens are often scarce.

FENNEL, ORANGE, AND PARSLEY SALAD

SERVES 4
PREP TIME: 20 MINUTES
TOTAL TIME: 20 MINUTES

- 2 medium fennel bulbs (8 ounces each)
- 5 medium oranges
- ⅔ cup fresh parsley leaves
- 2 tablespoons slivered pitted black olives
- 1 teaspoon olive oil
  Coarse salt and fresh ground pepper

1 Trim the fennel bulbs. Quarter, core, and thinly slice the bulbs crosswise.

2 Using a paring knife, remove the peel and pith from the oranges. Separate the oranges into segments over a large bowl (to catch the juices), then add the segments to the bowl.

3 Add the fennel, parsley, olives, and olive oil; season with salt and pepper. Gently toss, and serve.

Mango, hearts of palm, and fresh lime juice bring tropical flavors to the winter table. Try this salad before a meal of roasted or braised fish, or pan-fried steak or chops.

MANGO AND HEARTS OF PALM SALAD WITH LIME VINAIGRETTE

SERVES 4 ■ PREP TIME: 15 MINUTES ■ **TOTAL TIME: 15 MINUTES**

¼ cup fresh lime juice

4 teaspoons Dijon mustard

1 large mango, peeled, pitted, and cut into ½-inch wedges

½ small red onion, finely chopped

1 can (14.5 ounces) hearts of palm, drained, halved lengthwise, and cut into 1-inch pieces

Coarse salt and fresh ground pepper

1 head Boston lettuce (about 8 ounces), washed and dried

1 In a small bowl, whisk the lime juice and mustard. Set the vinaigrette aside.

2 In a medium bowl, toss the mango, onion, hearts of palm, and half the vinaigrette; season with salt and pepper.

3 Evenly divide the lettuce among 4 plates; top with the mango mixture. Season with additional salt and pepper, and drizzle with the remaining vinaigrette.

In this dish, the garlic tops serve as a roasting rack for the chicken. The garlic bottoms are then flipped halfway through the cooking time, to soak up the juices. Serve with toasted slices of French bread, if desired.

GARLIC-ROASTED CHICKEN BREASTS

SERVES 4 TO 6 ■ PREP TIME: 10 MINUTES ■ **TOTAL TIME: 1 HOUR 10 MINUTES**

4 heads garlic

8 sprigs fresh oregano

2 whole roaster chicken breasts (3½ pounds each), rinsed and patted dry

2 tablespoons olive oil

Coarse salt and fresh ground pepper

1 Preheat the oven to 400°F. Slice the tops from garlic heads, reserving the bottoms; arrange the tops, cut sides down, in the center of an 11-by-17-inch roasting pan. Place 1 sprig of the oregano over each garlic top, and arrange the chicken breasts over the garlic.

2 Place the reserved garlic bottoms, cut sides up, next to the chicken in the pan. Drizzle the chicken and garlic bottoms with the olive oil. Season the chicken with salt and pepper; place the remaining 4 sprigs of oregano on top.

3 Roast the chicken for 30 minutes; turn the garlic bottoms cut sides down, and rotate the pan. Continue roasting the chicken until the skin is browned, the juices run clear, and an instant-read thermometer inserted into the thickest part of the meat registers 165°F, about 30 minutes more.

4 Pour the pan juices into a measuring cup; skim the fat from the top. Serve the juices with the chicken and roasted garlic.

SAUTÉED BROCCOLI RABE

Coarse salt and fresh ground pepper

1½ pounds broccoli rabe, trimmed

3 tablespoons pine nuts

1 tablespoon olive oil

1 teaspoon grated lemon zest

In a large pot of boiling salted water, cook the broccoli rabe until bright green, 45 to 60 seconds. Drain; set aside. Toast the pine nuts in a skillet over medium heat, shaking the skillet, until evenly golden brown, 4 to 5 minutes; remove from the skillet. Heat the olive oil in the skillet. Add the broccoli rabe; cook, tossing occasionally, until heated through, 3 to 5 minutes, Toss the broccoli rabe with the pine nuts and lemon zest. Season with salt and pepper. Serve hot. **SERVES 4**

Saltimbocca, a classic Roman dish, provided the inspiration for this recipe. In our variation we replaced the traditional veal cutlets with chicken.

CHICKEN WITH PROSCIUTTO AND SAGE

SERVES 4 ■ PREP TIME: 10 MINUTES ■ **TOTAL TIME: 30 MINUTES**

¼ cup all-purpose flour
  Coarse salt and
  fresh ground pepper
4 fresh whole sage leaves, plus
  4 minced leaves
4 chicken cutlets
  (6 to 8 ounces each)
4 slices (3 ounces) thinly sliced
  prosciutto
4 teaspoons olive oil
¾ cup dry white wine
⅓ cup reduced-sodium canned
  chicken broth
1 tablespoon cold butter

1 In a shallow bowl, stir together the flour, ½ teaspoon salt, and ¼ teaspoon pepper. Set aside.

2 Lay 1 sage leaf lengthwise on each cutlet, then wrap a prosciutto slice around the middle of each cutlet, encasing the sage. Flatten with the palm of your hand to help the prosciutto adhere to the chicken. Dredge the cutlets in the seasoned flour; tap off excess.

3 In a large nonstick skillet, heat 2 teaspoons of the oil over medium-high heat. Cook 2 of the cutlets until golden brown and cooked through, 3 to 4 minutes per side. Remove the cutlets, and keep warm. Repeat with the remaining 2 teaspoons oil and 2 cutlets.

4 Add the wine and broth to the skillet; cook over high heat until reduced by three quarters, about 2 minutes. Remove from the heat; let cool for 1 minute. Add the butter and minced sage; stir until the butter is melted, about 30 seconds. Spoon the sauce onto plates; top with the cutlets. Serve immediately.

SAUTÉED SPINACH WITH GOLDEN RAISINS

1 tablespoon olive oil
1½ pounds trimmed spinach
¼ cup golden raisins
  Coarse salt and
  fresh ground pepper

In a large (12-inch) skillet, warm the oil. Cook the spinach in 3 additions, letting the first batch wilt before adding the next, and tossing often, until completely wilted, 3 to 4 minutes total. Stir in the raisins. Season with salt and pepper. **SERVES 4**

PREP TIME 10 MINUTES

For something a bit unexpected, here we filled enchiladas with chicken and scallions, then covered them with a spicy pumpkin sauce and Cheddar cheese.

ENCHILADAS WITH PUMPKIN SAUCE

SERVES 4 ■ PREP TIME: 20 MINUTES ■ **TOTAL TIME: 1 HOUR**

½ roast or rotisserie chicken (recipe for roast chicken on page 351), skin removed, meat shredded

6 scallions, thinly sliced

Coarse salt and fresh ground pepper

1 can (15 ounces) pumpkin purée

4 garlic cloves, peeled

1 jalapeño chile, quartered (remove ribs and seeds for less heat, if desired)

1 teaspoon chili powder

8 corn tortillas (6-inch)

1½ cups (6 ounces) grated sharp white Cheddar cheese

1 Preheat the oven to 425°F. In a medium bowl, combine the chicken and scallions. Season generously with salt and pepper; set aside.

2 In a blender, purée the pumpkin, garlic, jalapeño, chili powder, 2½ cups water, 2 teaspoons salt, and ¼ teaspoon pepper until smooth (hold the top firmly as the blender will be quite full). Pour 1 cup of the sauce in the bottom of an 8-inch square (or other shallow 2-quart) baking dish.

3 Lay the tortillas on a work surface; mound the chicken mixture on half of each tortilla, dividing evenly. Roll up each tortilla into a tight log; place seam side down over the sauce in the baking dish.

4 Pour the remaining sauce on top; sprinkle with the cheese. Place the dish on a baking sheet; bake until the cheese is golden and the sauce is bubbling, 25 to 30 minutes. Let cool for 5 minutes before serving.

PLANNING AHEAD
This dish can be assembled up to 8 hours ahead of time; refrigerate, covered with plastic wrap, until ready to bake (add a few minutes to the cooking time).

You can replace the zucchini with other vegetables, such as eggplant or bell peppers. Turmeric, which is related to ginger, is what gives curries and prepared mustard their distinctive yellow color. Look for it in the supermarket's spice aisle.

MOROCCAN CHICKEN COUSCOUS

SERVES 4 ■ PREP TIME: 30 MINUTES ■ TOTAL TIME: 45 MINUTES

8 bone-in, skinless chicken thighs (about 2½ pounds)

3 carrots, cut into 1½-inch chunks

3 onions, thinly sliced

1 (14.5-ounce) can whole tomatoes, drained

1 (15.5-ounce) can chickpeas, drained and rinsed

1¾ cups reduced-sodium chicken broth

½ teaspoon ground ginger

¼ teaspoon ground turmeric

¼ teaspoon ground cinnamon

⅛ teaspoon chili powder

Coarse salt and fresh ground pepper

2 zucchini (about 1 pound), halved crosswise and quartered lengthwise

Couscous, for serving (recipe page 359)

1 In a Dutch oven (or other 5-quart pot with a tight-fitting lid), combine the chicken, carrots, onions, tomatoes, chickpeas, stock, ¾ cup water, the ginger, turmeric, cinnamon, chili powder, 1 teaspoon salt, and ⅛ teaspoon pepper. Break up the tomatoes with a spoon.

2 Bring to a simmer over medium heat. Cover, and cook for 15 minutes. Add the zucchini, and cook until the chicken is cooked through, yet still tender, about 15 minutes more.

3 Divide the couscous evenly among 4 bowls. Spoon the chicken, vegetables, and broth on top. Serve immediately.

Curries can be quite mild or extremely spicy. It all depends on the type of curry powder that is used to make them—and how much is added. Feel free to adjust the recipe according to your own taste.

CHICKEN CURRY

SERVES 4 ■ PREP TIME: 20 MINUTES ■ **TOTAL TIME: 45 MINUTES**

2 tablespoons all-purpose flour

4 boneless, skinless chicken breast halves (6 ounces each)

1 tablespoon plus 2 teaspoons olive oil

1 medium onion, finely chopped (¾ cup)

2 garlic cloves, minced

2 teaspoons medium to hot curry powder

Coarse salt

¾ pound small red potatoes, cut into ½-inch chunks

1 can (14.5 ounces) diced tomatoes (preferably zesty flavored), with juice

Suggested accompaniments

Rice

Plain yogurt

Raisins

Toasted almonds

Store-bought mango chutney

1 Place the flour on a plate. Dredge the chicken in the flour, shaking off excess. In a large nonstick skillet, heat the 1 tablespoon oil over medium heat. Add the chicken, and cook until golden brown, about 3 minutes per side. Transfer the chicken to a bowl; set aside.

2 Heat the remaining 2 teaspoons oil in the same skillet; cook the onion and garlic, stirring frequently, until the onion is softened, about 5 minutes. Stir in the curry powder and ¾ teaspoon salt; cook for 1 minute more.

3 Add the potatoes and 1 cup water; bring to a boil. Reduce the heat to a simmer; cover, and cook until the potatoes are just tender but still offer slight resistance when pierced with the tip of a paring knife, about 7 minutes. Stir in the tomatoes and ¼ cup water.

4 Return the chicken to the skillet along with any accumulated juices in the bowl; simmer, covered, until the chicken is cooked through, 12 to 15 minutes. Serve hot, with desired accompaniments on the side.

A generous amount of carrots adds a sweet earthy taste to these chicken breasts. Using prunes lends additional rich flavor, and is a variation of popular Mediterranean dishes that combine poultry or meat with dried fruit.

ROASTED CHICKEN BREASTS WITH CARROTS AND ONION

SERVES 4 ■ PREP TIME: 15 MINUTES ■ **TOTAL TIME: 45 MINUTES**

4 bone-in chicken breast halves (10 to 12 ounces each)

1 pound carrots, peeled, halved lengthwise, and cut diagonally into ½-inch chunks

6 garlic cloves, quartered

1 medium red onion, halved, cut into ½-inch wedges

Coarse salt and fresh ground pepper

¾ cup pitted prunes, quartered lengthwise

Couscous, for serving (recipe page 359; optional)

1 Preheat the oven to 450°F. Place the chicken on a rimmed baking sheet. Arrange the carrots, garlic, and onion around the chicken; season the chicken and vegetables generously with salt and pepper. Roast for 10 minutes.

2 Toss the prunes with the vegetables. Continue roasting until the chicken is cooked through and the vegetables are tender, 15 to 20 minutes more. Serve the chicken and vegetables over the couscous, if desired.

Creamy polenta provides a wonderful counterpoint to this hearty stew. To time everything right, bring the water to a boil while the chicken is browning, then add the polenta to the water when beginning step three of the chicken recipe.

MEDITERRANEAN CHICKEN STEW

SERVES 4 ■ PREP TIME: 30 MINUTES ■ **TOTAL TIME: 30 MINUTES**

1½ pounds boneless, skinless chicken breast halves, cut into ¾-inch chunks

Coarse salt and fresh ground pepper

3 teaspoons olive oil

4 garlic cloves, minced

1 can (15.5 ounces) chickpeas, drained and rinsed

4 plum tomatoes, cored and cut into ½-inch pieces (2 cups)

2 tablespoons chopped pitted kalamata olives (about 5)

1 teaspoon white-wine vinegar

¼ cup chopped fresh parsley

Polenta (recipe page 360), for serving

1 Season the chicken with 1 teaspoon salt and ¼ teaspoon pepper. In a large nonstick skillet, heat 2 teaspoons of the oil over medium-high heat. Add the chicken, and cook, turning occasionally, until golden, 3 to 4 minutes. Transfer to a plate.

2 Reduce the heat to medium-low; add the remaining teaspoon oil to the skillet. Add the garlic, and cook, stirring, until fragrant, about 30 seconds. Add the chickpeas and 1 cup water. Bring to a boil; cook until the liquid is reduced by half, about 2 minutes.

3 Add the tomatoes; cook over medium heat until starting to break down, 3 to 4 minutes. Add the olives, vinegar, and chicken along with any accumulated juices to the pan; toss until warmed through, about 1 minute. Stir in the parsley. Serve over the polenta.

SUBSTITUTING WITH SHRIMP
This recipe can also be made with 1½ pounds peeled and deveined shrimp instead of chicken; replace the chick peas with cannellini beans.

Grated apples are an unusual but welcome addition to yogurt sauce. Ours is a variation on raita, the traditional accompaniment to many Indian dishes; its cooling effect counterbalances the spiciness of the meat.

TANDOORI CHICKEN WITH YOGURT SAUCE

SERVES 4
PREP TIME: 30 MINUTES
TOTAL TIME: 35 MINUTES

- 1 cup plain low-fat yogurt
- 2 garlic cloves, minced
- 1 teaspoon ground turmeric
- 1 teaspoon ground ginger
  Coarse salt and fresh ground pepper
- 4 bone-in, skinless chicken breast halves (10 to 12 ounces each)
- 2 Granny Smith apples
- 1 tablespoon chopped fresh cilantro

1 Preheat the oven to 475°F. In a large bowl, mix together ½ cup of the yogurt, the garlic, turmeric, ginger, 2 teaspoons salt, and ¼ teaspoon pepper. Add the chicken; turn to coat.

2 Transfer the chicken to a rimmed baking sheet. Roast until an instant-read thermometer inserted in the thickest part of the breast (avoiding the bone) registers 160°F, 25 to 30 minutes.

3 Meanwhile, peel the apple; coarsely grate into a medium bowl. Add the cilantro and the remaining ½ cup yogurt; season with salt and pepper. Serve the sauce alongside the chicken, with rice, if desired.

Thyme and sage give this sauce savory flavor, to complement the tartness of the cranberries. Loaded with antioxidants and vitamin C, cranberries are believed to help boost the immune system.

CHICKEN WITH CRANBERRY SAUCE

SERVES 4 ■ PREP TIME: 10 MINUTES ■ **TOTAL TIME: 40 MINUTES**

2 tablespoons butter

1½ teaspoons dried thyme

Coarse salt and fresh ground pepper

4 bone-in chicken breast halves (8 ounces each)

1 medium onion, finely chopped (about 1 cup)

½ teaspoon dried sage

2 cups reduced-sodium chicken broth

1 cup cranberries

¼ cup sugar

1 teaspoon cornstarch mixed with 1 tablespoon water

1 Preheat the oven to 450°F. In a small bowl, mix 1 tablespoon of the butter, 1 teaspoon of the thyme, ½ teaspoon salt, and ¼ teaspoon pepper. Rub evenly under the chicken skin. Place on a rimmed baking sheet; roast skin side up until the skin is golden brown and the meat is cooked through, about 25 minutes.

2 Meanwhile, melt the remaining tablespoon butter in a large saucepan over medium heat. Cook the onion, stirring occasionally, until golden, about 8 minutes. Add the sage and the remaining ½ teaspoon thyme; cook for 1 minute. Add the broth; simmer until reduced to 1½ cups, 10 to 15 minutes. Strain the mixture; return to the saucepan.

3 Add the cranberries and sugar; boil until the berries burst, 5 to 8 minutes. Whisk in the cornstarch mixture; return to a boil. Cook until slightly thickened, 1 to 2 minutes. Remove from the heat (the sauce will thicken as it stands). Season with salt and pepper. To serve, spoon the sauce over the chicken.

MASHED WHITE BEANS

1 tablespoon olive oil

2 garlic cloves, minced

2 cans (19 ounces each) cannellini beans, drained and rinsed

1 tablespoon chopped fresh sage (or 1 teaspoon dried)

Coarse salt and fresh ground pepper

1 In a large skillet, heat the olive oil over medium heat. Cook the garlic, stirring often, until golden, about 1 minute.

2 Add the beans, sage, and 1¼ cups water. Cook, stirring often, until the beans are hot and the liquid thickens, about 4 minutes.

3 Mash the beans, leaving some whole. Season with salt and pepper. **SERVES 4**

Here's a tried-and-true winter roast, with a straightforward (and quick) preparation and a side of potatoes. You need only green beans to create a complete meal, but if you want to add another side dish, try the Swiss chard on page 249.

ROAST BEEF WITH SHALLOTS AND NEW POTATOES

SERVES 4 ■ PREP TIME: 15 MINUTES ■ **TOTAL TIME: 1 HOUR**

1½ pounds small red new potatoes (10 to 12), halved, or quartered if large

1 pound shallots (8 to 10), peeled and trimmed, halved lengthwise

2 tablespoons olive oil

Coarse salt and fresh ground pepper

1½ pounds eye-of-round beef roast, tied

1 Preheat the oven to 400°F. On a large, rimmed baking sheet, toss the potatoes and shallots with the oil; season with salt and pepper.

2 Push the potatoes and shallots toward the edges of the baking sheet; place the roast in the center. Turn the roast to coat with the oil on the pan and season generously with salt and pepper.

3 Roast, tossing the potatoes and shallots occasionally, until an instant-read thermometer inserted in the center of the beef registers 130°F (for medium-rare), 40 to 50 minutes. Let the beef rest, loosely covered with aluminum foil, before slicing and serving with the potatoes and shallots.

LEMON-THYME GREEN BEANS

Coarse salt and fresh ground pepper

1½ pounds green beans, ends trimmed

3 tablespoons fresh lemon juice (from about 1 lemon)

2 tablespoons butter

1 teaspoon fresh thyme leaves, plus more for garnish (optional)

1 In a large skillet with a tight-fitting lid, bring ½ inch water to a boil; salt generously.

2 Add the green beans; reduce to a simmer, and cover the skillet. Steam the beans, tossing occasionally, until crisp-tender, 6 to 10 minutes.

3 Pull the lid back slightly, and tilt the skillet to drain the water from the green beans; add the lemon juice, butter, and thyme. Season with salt and pepper, and toss to melt butter. Serve the green beans garnished with additional thyme, if desired. **SERVES 4**

We like to prepare these steaks in the broiler throughout the winter months, but you can also prepare them any time on an outdoor grill or in a grill pan.

CHILI-RUBBED SKIRT STEAK

SERVES: 4 ■ PREP TIME: 20 MINUTES ■ TOTAL TIME: 30 MINUTES

2 teaspoons chili powder
1 teaspoon ground coriander
1 teaspoon light brown sugar
½ teaspoon dried oregano
Coarse salt and
fresh ground pepper
1¼ to 1½ pounds beef skirt steak,
cut into 4 pieces
1½ teaspoons olive oil

1 Heat the broiler with the rack 4 inches from the heat. In a small bowl, combine the chili powder, coriander, sugar, oregano, 1½ teaspoons salt, and ¼ teaspoon pepper. Coat the steaks evenly on both sides with the oil, then the spice mixture, patting to help the mixture adhere.

2 Place the steaks on a rimmed baking sheet or broiler pan. Broil the steaks, without turning, until medium-rare, 5 to 8 minutes, depending on the thickness. Transfer the steaks to a large platter and cover with aluminum foil; let rest for 10 minutes.

3 Remove foil and divide steaks among 4 serving plates. Drizzle with any accumulated juices from the platter.

ROMAINE HEART SALAD WITH CREAMY CHILI DRESSING

¼ cup reduced-fat sour cream
2 tablespoons light mayonnaise
2 tablespoons fresh lemon juice
1 teaspoon chili powder
Coarse salt and
fresh ground pepper
2 heads romaine lettuce
¼ cup chopped scallions

In a medium bowl, place the sour cream, mayonnaise, lemon juice, and chili powder; season with salt and pepper. Whisk to combine. Remove the dark outer leaves from each head of romaine, leaving the heart; place leaves in a plastic bag lined with a paper towel and refrigerate for another use. Slice the hearts in half lengthwise. Place one half on each plate; top with the dressing. Sprinkle with the scallions and serve.
SERVES 4

PREP TIME | **20** MINUTES

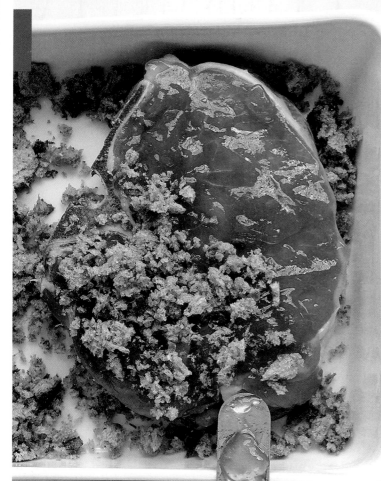

There's no need to fry in a lot of oil to get a crisp breadcrumb crust. Before baking, moisten the crumbs with a little oil; coat the pork, chicken, or fish, and bake until golden.

CRISPY APRICOT PORK CHOPS

SERVES 4
PREP TIME: 10 MINUTES
TOTAL TIME: 30 MINUTES

- 1 tablespoon olive oil, plus more for baking sheet
- 2 slices multigrain sandwich bread
- 4 bone-in pork loin chops (about 8 ounces each, ¾ to 1 inch thick), patted dry
  Coarse salt and fresh ground pepper
- 4 teaspoons apricot jam

1 Preheat the oven to 425°F. Lightly brush a rimmed baking sheet with oil; set aside.

2 Tear the bread into large pieces; place in a food processor. Pulse until large crumbs form. Drizzle with the oil; pulse once or twice, just until the crumbs are moistened (you should have about 1½ cups crumbs).

3 Season the pork chops generously with salt and pepper; spread one side of each chop with 1 teaspoon jam. Dividing evenly, sprinkle the breadcrumbs over the jam, and pat them on gently.

4 Transfer the pork, coated side up, to the prepared baking sheet. Bake until the crust is golden and the pork is opaque throughout (the meat should register 150°F on an instant-read thermometer), 14 to 16 minutes. Serve immediately.

PREP TIME **10** MINUTES

**BABY BROCCOLI
WITH ORANGE SAUCE**
Recipe page 330

PREP TIME | **10** MINUTES

Try these flavorful chops with Buttermilk Mashed Potatoes (page 247), Roasted Pears and Sweet Potatoes (page 249), or Roasted Fennel (page 247).

LEMON-PARSLEY PORK CHOPS

SERVES 4 ■ PREP TIME: 10 MINUTES ■ TOTAL TIME: 25 MINUTES

1 lemon, zest removed and minced (see note below)

2 tablespoons chopped fresh parsley

1 garlic clove, minced

Coarse salt and fresh ground pepper

2 tablespoons olive oil

4 bone-in loin pork chops (about 8 ounces each)

1 Combine the minced lemon in a small bowl with the parsley, garlic, ½ teaspoon coarse salt, and ¼ teaspoon ground pepper. Set aside.

2 Heat the olive oil in a large skillet over high heat. Season the pork chops on both sides with salt and pepper. Cook in the skillet until browned, 2 to 3 minutes per side.

3 Add ½ cup water to the skillet; bring to a boil. Reduce the heat to medium-low; cover, and simmer gently until the pork is cooked through, 8 to 10 minutes. Transfer the pork chops to a platter or serving plates; drizzle with the pan juices as desired, and sprinkle with the lemon-parsley mixture.

MINCING LEMON ZEST
With a vegetable peeler, remove the lemon zest in long strips (avoid the bitter white pith). Use a sharp knife to cut the zest into thinner strips, then finely cut crosswise.

Sautéed Bok Choy and Broccoli (page 249) and a big bowl of white rice are all you need to accompany these tasty—and remarkably easy—fish steaks.

SALMON STEAKS WITH HOISIN GLAZE

SERVES 4 ■ PREP TIME: 5 MINUTES ■ **TOTAL TIME: 18 MINUTES**

1 tablespoon fresh orange juice
2 tablespoons hoisin sauce
2 teaspoons honey
4 salmon steaks (each 8 to 10 ounces and 1 inch thick)
  Coarse salt and fresh ground pepper

1 Heat the broiler. In a small bowl, whisk together the orange juice, hoisin sauce, and honey to make a glaze.

2 Rinse the salmon steaks, and pat dry. Season both sides with salt and pepper. Place the steaks on a rimmed baking sheet. Brush generously with the glaze.

3 Broil the salmon about 4 inches from the heat source, basting once, until opaque in the center, 10 to 13 minutes.

Lemon slices help keep the fish fillets moist during cooking. For a simple sauce, we combined lemon juice, white wine, and butter.

SOLE WITH LEMON-BUTTER SAUCE

SERVES 4 ■ PREP TIME: 10 MINUTES ■ TOTAL TIME: 20 MINUTES

½ cup dry white wine

8 sole fillets (3 to 4 ounces each)
  Coarse salt and
  fresh ground pepper

16 very thin lemon slices (from
  1 to 2 lemons), seeds removed
  Juice of 1 lemon (3 tablespoons)

3 tablespoons cold butter,
  cut into pieces
  Dill sprigs (optional)

1 Place the wine in a large, lidded skillet. Fold each sole fillet into thirds. Arrange in the skillet; season with salt and pepper. Lay two overlapping lemon slices on each piece of fish.

2 Bring the wine to a boil; reduce the heat to medium-low. Cover; simmer gently until the fish is opaque throughout, 3 to 5 minutes. With a spatula, transfer the fish to serving plates.

3 Return the liquid in the skillet to a boil; cook until reduced to ⅓ cup, 1 to 2 minutes. Add the lemon juice; remove from the heat. Whisk in the butter until smooth. Season with salt; strain, if desired. Serve with the fish; garnish with fresh dill and pepper, if desired.

This main course needs no accompaniment other than a tossed green salad. Try the Mixed Green Salad with Citrus Dressing on page 54.

COD WITH FENNEL AND POTATOES

SERVES 4 ■ PREP TIME: 15 MINUTES ■ **TOTAL TIME: 40 MINUTES**

- 1 tablespoon olive oil
- 1 small onion, diced
- 3 garlic cloves, minced
- 1 trimmed fennel bulb (reserve fronds), cut into ½-inch pieces
- 1 pound russet potatoes, peeled, halved lengthwise, and thinly sliced
- 1 can (14.5 ounces) reduced-sodium chicken broth
- 2 tablespoons tomato paste
- 3 strips (½ inch wide) orange zest
  Coarse salt
- 4 boneless, skinless cod fillets (6 ounces each)

1 In a 12-inch skillet, heat the olive oil over medium heat. Add the onion and garlic. Cook, stirring frequently, until the onion is soft, about 7 minutes.

2 Add the chopped fennel; cook, stirring frequently, until crisp-tender, about 5 minutes.

3 Add the potatoes, chicken broth, tomato paste, and orange zest; season with salt. Boil for 10 minutes.

4 Place the cod fillets on top; reduce the heat. Cover; simmer until the fish is opaque throughout, about 10 minutes. Serve with the chopped reserved fennel fronds.

Like the asparagus tart that's a harbinger of spring (see page 69), this mushroom-topped variation is a crowd-pleaser. It makes a lovely dinner, or, when cut into bite-size pieces, a perfect hors d'oeuvre for a cocktail party.

MUSHROOM TART

SERVES 4 ▪ PREP TIME: 45 MINUTES ▪ **TOTAL TIME: 45 MINUTES**

Flour for rolling out puff pastry

1 sheet frozen puff pastry (from a 17.3-ounce package), thawed according to package instructions

1 medium onion, halved and thinly sliced

2 tablespoons olive oil

Coarse salt and fresh ground pepper

2 packages (10 ounces each) white mushrooms, trimmed and thinly sliced

1 package (10 ounces) fresh baby spinach

2 ounces soft goat cheese, crumbled

1 Preheat the oven to 400°F. On a floured surface, roll the puff pastry out to a 16-by-10-inch rectangle. Trim uneven edges. Place the pastry on a baking sheet. With a sharp knife, lightly score the dough to form a 1-inch border. Using a fork, prick the dough inside the border every ½ inch. Bake until golden, rotating the pan once, about 15 minutes.

2 Meanwhile, in a small saucepan with a tight-fitting lid, toss the onion with 1 tablespoon of the oil. Season with salt. Cover and cook over medium heat until the onion begins to brown, about 5 minutes. Stir. Continue cooking with the cover on for 15 minutes, stirring every 5 minutes. Set aside.

3 In a large saucepan with a tight-fitting lid, heat the remaining tablespoon of oil. Add the mushrooms; cover and cook until tender and all liquid has evaporated, about 10 minutes. Fold in the spinach; season with salt and pepper. Cover and cook until wilted, about 5 minutes more. Drain any liquid.

4 Top the dough with the mushroom-spinach mixture. Scatter the onions and goat cheese on top. Bake until the cheese is lightly browned, about 15 minutes.

PREP TIME **45** MINUTES

Rather than eliminating yolks altogether, we used fewer—to reduce fat and to avoid the rubbery texture that can be obtained by using only egg whites.

POTATO AND ONION FRITTATA

SERVES 4 ■ PREP TIME: 15 MINUTES ■ **TOTAL TIME: 45 MINUTES**

2 tablespoons olive oil

1 large onion, halved and thinly sliced

1 baking potato (8 ounces), peeled and thinly sliced

½ teaspoon dried rosemary, crumbled

Coarse salt and fresh ground pepper

5 large eggs

5 large egg whites

½ cup whole flat-leaf parsley leaves

BELL PEPPER SAUTÉ

2 bell peppers, red, yellow, or both

1 tablespoon olive oil

½ small red onion, diced

Coarse salt and fresh ground pepper

Remove the seeds and ribs from the peppers; cut lengthwise into strips and halve crosswise. Heat the oil in a large nonstick skillet over medium heat. Add the peppers and onion; season with salt and pepper. Cook, stirring occasionally, until the peppers are just tender, about 10 minutes.
SERVES 4

1 In a medium (10-inch) nonstick broiler-proof skillet, heat 1 tablespoon of the oil over medium heat. Add the onion, potato, and rosemary; season with salt and pepper, and toss to combine.

2 Cover the skillet, and cook for 10 minutes; uncover. Cook, tossing the mixture occasionally, until the onion and potato are tender, about 5 minutes.

3 Meanwhile, in a medium bowl, whisk together the eggs, egg whites, parsley leaves, ¾ teaspoon salt, and ¼ teaspoon pepper.

4 Heat the broiler with a rack set 4 inches from the heat. Add the remaining tablespoon oil to the vegetables in the skillet. Pour the egg mixture into the skillet.

5 Cook on the stove, over low heat, lifting the mixture a few times around the edges with a spatula to let egg flow underneath. Continue cooking until the frittata is almost set in the center, about 10 minutes.

6 Place the skillet under the broiler; broil until the frittata is set and the top is lightly golden, about 3 minutes. Run a clean spatula around the edges to loosen, then slide the frittata out onto a serving plate, and cut into wedges.

Because these crispy bean cakes are broiled rather than fried, the recipe doesn't call for much oil, so the cakes contain less fat; they are also easier to prepare than fried versions.

SPICY BLACK-BEAN CAKES

SERVES 4 ■ PREP TIME: 20 MINUTES ■ TOTAL TIME: 30 MINUTES

2 tablespoons olive oil

4 scallions, thinly sliced

6 garlic cloves, pressed

1 to 2 jalapeño chiles, finely chopped (ribs and seeds removed for less heat, if desired)

1 tablespoon ground cumin

2 cans (15.5 ounces each) black beans, drained and rinsed

Coarse salt and fresh ground pepper

1 large sweet potato, peeled and coarsely grated (2 cups)

1 large egg, lightly beaten

½ cup plain dried breadcrumbs

Lime Sour Cream (recipe below)

1 Heat the broiler. In a small skillet over medium heat, warm 1 tablespoon of the oil. Cook the scallions until softened, 1 minute. Add the garlic, jalapeño, and cumin; cook until fragrant, 30 seconds. Transfer to a large bowl.

2 Add the beans to the bowl; mash with a fork or a potato masher, leaving about one quarter of the beans whole. Season generously with salt and pepper. Fold in the sweet potato, egg, and breadcrumbs. Divide into 8 balls of equal size; flatten into patties.

3 Brush a baking sheet with the remaining tablespoon oil; place the patties on the sheet, ½ inch apart. Broil 4 inches from the heat until golden brown, 8 to 10 minutes. With a thin metal spatula, carefully turn the cakes. Broil until crisp, 2 to 3 minutes more. Serve with the lime sour cream.

EASY GRATING
If you want to grate the potatoes with a box grater (instead of a food processor), use the large holes, and work over a bowl.

LIME SOUR CREAM

½ cup reduced-fat sour cream

2 teaspoons fresh lime juice

1 small jalapeño chile, minced (ribs and seeds removed for less heat, if desired)

Coarse salt

In a small bowl, combine the sour cream with the lime juice and jalapeño; season with salt.

Baking pasta with cheese on top creates a chewy and crispy topping kids will love. You can assemble the dish ahead and refrigerate it, then bake it right before dinner.

BAKED RAVIOLI

SERVES 4 TO 6 ■ PREP TIME: 25 MINUTES ■ **TOTAL TIME: 50 MINUTES**

2 tablespoons olive oil

1 medium onion, chopped

3 garlic cloves, minced
  Coarse salt and
  fresh ground pepper

1½ teaspoons dried thyme or
  oregano

1 can (28 ounces) whole tomatoes

1 can (28 ounces) crushed
  tomatoes

2 pounds ravioli

1½ cups shredded mozzarella

½ cup grated Parmesan

1 Preheat the oven to 425°F. Heat the oil in a large saucepan over medium heat. Add the onion and garlic, and season with salt and pepper; cook, stirring occasionally, until softened, about 5 minutes. Add the thyme and tomatoes. Bring to a boil, reduce heat, and simmer, breaking up the tomatoes with a spoon, until the sauce is thickened and reduced to about 5½ cups, 20 to 25 minutes.

2 Meanwhile, cook the ravioli in a large pot of boiling salted water just until they float to the top (the pasta will continue to cook in the oven). Drain the pasta; return to the pot.

3 Toss the sauce with the pasta. Pour the pasta into a large gratin dish or 9-by-13-inch baking dish, and sprinkle with the cheeses. Bake until golden, 20 to 25 minutes. Cool slightly before serving.

SUBSTITUTING SPAGHETTI
Try this recipe with a pound of spaghetti (cook a few minutes less than the package instructions direct). Don't worry if it seems like there's too much sauce; it will be absorbed as the pasta bakes.

The sauce for this dish can be made a day or two ahead (keep the bacon separate) and refrigerated. Gently reheat as the pasta boils; add the bacon to the sauce during the last few minutes of heating.

MUSHROOM RAGOUT WITH PASTA

SERVES 6 ■ PREP TIME: 30 MINUTES ■ **TOTAL TIME: 1 HOUR**

4 slices bacon, cut crosswise into ½-inch pieces

1 small onion, finely chopped

2 packages (10 ounces each) cremini mushrooms, trimmed and quartered

2 packages (10 ounces each) white mushrooms, trimmed and quartered

¼ cup tomato paste

2 teaspoons dried thyme

¼ cup chopped fresh parsley

2 teaspoons red-wine vinegar

¾ pound spaghetti

Shaved Parmesan cheese, for garnish (optional)

1 In a large 5-quart saucepan with a tight-fitting lid (that will be used later), cook the bacon over medium heat, uncovered, stirring until crispy, about 5 minutes. With a slotted spoon, transfer to a paper towel to drain. Set aside.

2 Add the onion to the saucepan; stir until golden, about 1 minute. Add the mushrooms; cover. Cook until the juices have evaporated, about 20 minutes.

3 Stir in the tomato paste, thyme, and 2 cups water until combined; cover. Cook until the sauce has thickened, 10 to 15 minutes. Stir in the parsley and vinegar. Add the bacon, reserving some for garnish, if desired.

4 Meanwhile, cook the pasta until al dente according to the package instructions. Drain and return to the pot.

5 To serve, toss the pasta with the ragout. Garnish with the reserved bacon and shaved Parmesan, if desired. Serve immediately.

PREP TIME | **30** MINUTES

Two types of Cheddar are used in this recipe. If you like, use just one type, or mix Cheddar with another melting cheese, such as pepper Jack, Muenster, Swiss, or mozzarella.

MACARONI AND CHEESE

SERVES 8 ■ PREP TIME: 30 MINUTES ■ **TOTAL TIME: 1 HOUR**

1 pound elbow pasta
4 tablespoons butter
1 small onion, chopped
¼ cup all-purpose flour (spooned and leveled)
4 cups milk
⅛ teaspoon cayenne pepper (optional)
1¼ cups (5 ounces) shredded yellow Cheddar cheese
1¼ cups (5 ounces) shredded white Cheddar cheese
Coarse salt and fresh ground pepper
8 ounces ham, diced into ½-inch pieces
2 slices white sandwich bread

1 Preheat the oven to 375°F. Cook the pasta according to package instructions; drain and reserve. Meanwhile, in a 5-quart heavy pot, melt the butter over medium heat. Add the onion; cook, stirring occasionally, until softened, 3 to 5 minutes. Whisk in the flour to coat the onion. In a slow, steady stream, whisk in the milk until there are no lumps.

2 Cook, whisking often, until the mixture is thick and bubbly and coats the back of a wooden spoon, 6 to 8 minutes. Stir in the cayenne, if using, and 1 cup each of the yellow and white Cheddar cheese. Season with 1 teaspoon salt and ¼ teaspoon pepper.

3 Toss the pasta with the cheese mixture; fold in the ham. Transfer to a 9-by-13-inch baking dish or individual dishes (see below). Set aside.

4 In a food processor, pulse the bread until large crumbs form. Toss together with the remaining ¼ cup each white and yellow Cheddar, and ¼ teaspoon salt. Top the pasta with the breadcrumb mixture. Bake until the top is golden, about 30 minutes.

MAKING INDIVIDUAL SERVINGS
This recipe makes enough to fill eight 12-to-16-ounce baking dishes. Divide the macaroni and cheese evenly, sprinkle with topping, and bake for 15 to 20 minutes, until golden.

Orecchiette are small ear-shaped pasta shells; fusilli or farfalle can be used instead. You can also replace the arugula with two cups whole fresh flat-leaf parsley leaves.

PASTA WITH LENTILS AND ARUGULA

SERVES 6 ■ PREP TIME: 35 MINUTES ■ **TOTAL TIME: 45 MINUTES**

2 tablespoons olive oil

2 large onions, halved and thinly sliced (4 cups)

Coarse salt and fresh ground pepper

12 ounces plum tomatoes, cored and diced (about 2 cups)

¾ cup lentils, picked over and rinsed

12 ounces orecchiette pasta

1 bunch (8 ounces) arugula, stemmed and coarsely chopped

½ cup finely grated Parmesan cheese, plus more for serving (optional)

1 Heat the oil in a large skillet over medium-low heat. Add the onions and ½ teaspoon salt; cover, and cook until the onions wilt, about 20 minutes. Uncover; raise the heat to medium. Cook, stirring often, until the onions are dark brown, 20 to 25 minutes more.

2 Add ¼ cup water; stir to loosen any browned bits from the pan. Stir in the tomatoes; remove from the heat.

3 Meanwhile, in a medium saucepan, cover the lentils with water by 1 inch. Bring to a simmer. Cover; cook until the lentils are tender but still holding their shape, 15 to 20 minutes. Drain; stir into the onion mixture. Season with salt and pepper.

4 In a pot of salted water, cook the pasta until al dente according to the package instructions. Reserve 1 cup of the pasta water; drain the pasta, and return it to the pot.

5 Add the lentil mixture, arugula, cheese, and reserved pasta water; toss. Season with salt and pepper. Serve with more cheese, if desired.

CLEANING ARUGULA
Before using, always wash arugula well in several changes of cold water, until you no longer see any grit in the bottom of the bowl.

PREP TIME | **30** MINUTES

A traditional carbonara sauce is typically made with bacon, eggs, and cheese. We've added a little half-and-half for a more silky texture.

SPAGHETTI CARBONARA

SERVES 4
PREP TIME: 30 MINUTES
TOTAL TIME: 30 MINUTES

8 ounces bacon (8 slices), cut 1 inch thick crosswise

Coarse salt and fresh ground pepper

1 pound spaghetti

3 large eggs

¾ cup grated Parmesan cheese, plus more for serving

½ cup half-and-half

1 Set a large pot of water to boil (for the pasta). In a large skillet, cook the bacon over medium heat, stirring occasionally, until crisp, 8 to 12 minutes; transfer to a paper-towel-lined plate.

2 Salt the boiling water generously; add the pasta and cook until al dente according to the package instructions.

3 Meanwhile, in a large bowl, whisk together the eggs, Parmesan, and half-and-half. Set aside.

4 Drain the pasta, leaving some water clinging to it. Working quickly, add the hot pasta to the egg mixture. Add the bacon; season with salt and pepper, and toss all to combine (the heat from the pasta will cook the eggs). Serve immediately, sprinkled with additional Parmesan cheese.

Because preparing fresh squash can be time-consuming, we used frozen squash as a shortcut here. You can substitute an equal amount of puréed fresh squash (see note below).

BAKED SHELLS WITH WINTER SQUASH

SERVES 6 ■ PREP TIME: 10 MINUTES ■ TOTAL TIME: 50 MINUTES

Butter for the baking dish

4 tablespoons olive oil

2 large onions, halved and thinly sliced

Coarse salt and fresh ground pepper

2 teaspoons chopped fresh rosemary leaves

1 pound small pasta shells

1 package (12 ounces) frozen winter squash purée, thawed

1 cup grated Parmesan cheese

3 slices crusty baguette, cut into ¼-inch cubes (1½ cups)

1 Preheat the oven to 400°F. Butter a 9-by-13-inch baking dish. Heat 3 tablespoons of the oil in a large skillet over medium-low heat. Add the onions; season with salt and pepper. Cover; cook until the onions are soft and release their liquid, about 15 minutes. Uncover; raise the heat to medium. Cook, stirring, until the onions are browned, 20 to 25 minutes. Stir in 1 teaspoon of the rosemary.

2 Meanwhile, cook the pasta in a large pot of boiling salted water for 2 minutes less than the package instructions suggest. Drain, reserving 1½ cups of the cooking water. Return the pasta to the pot.

3 Stir squash and reserved pasta water into the onions; simmer for 2 minutes. Toss the squash mixture and ½ cup of the Parmesan with the pasta. Transfer to the prepared dish.

4 Combine the bread cubes with the remaining Parmesan, rosemary, and oil; season with salt and pepper. Top the pasta with the bread cubes; bake until golden brown, 10 to 15 minutes.

SUBSTITUTING FRESH SQUASH
Roast whole winter squash on a rimmed baking sheet, turning occasionally, until very tender when pierced with a knife, about 1 hour, depending on the size of the squash. When cool enough to handle, halve the squash lengthwise and scrape the flesh into a food processor (discard the skin and seeds). Purée until smooth. You will need 2 cups (from about ¾ pound squash).

We love the way this toss-and-serve pasta dish is put together so easily. Try the Fennel, Orange, and Parsley Salad (page 271) as a starter.

RIGATONI WITH SAUSAGE AND PARSLEY

SERVES 6 ■ PREP TIME: 30 MINUTES ■ **TOTAL TIME: 30 MINUTES**

1 pound bulk spicy Italian sausage, removed from casings and crumbled

2 medium red onions, halved and sliced ¼-inch thick

1 can (14.5 ounces) reduced-sodium chicken broth

Coarse salt and fresh ground pepper

1 pound rigatoni (or other short tubular pasta)

3 cups packed fresh flat-leaf parsley leaves

½ cup grated Parmesan cheese, plus more for garnish, if desired

1 In a large nonstick skillet over medium-high heat, cook the sausage until browned, breaking apart any large pieces with a wooden spoon, about 5 minutes. Reduce the heat to medium. Add the onions; cook, stirring occasionally, until the onions are caramelized and the sausage is cooked through, 10 to 12 minutes. Add the broth; cook until heated through, 3 to 5 minutes.

2 Meanwhile, in a large pot of boiling salted water, cook the pasta until al dente according to the package instructions. Drain; return to the pot.

3 Add the sausage mixture, parsley, and Parmesan to the pasta; toss to combine. Season with salt and pepper.

To make meatballs that are moist and tender, avoid using very lean ground turkey. For convenience, make a batch of sauce and meatballs ahead and freeze for up to three months.

SPAGHETTI WITH TURKEY MEATBALLS

SERVES 6 ■ PREP TIME: 50 MINUTES ■ **TOTAL TIME: 1 HOUR**

3 tablespoons olive oil

4 garlic cloves, minced

5 cups canned crushed tomatoes

½ teaspoon dried oregano

¼ teaspoon dried thyme

Coarse salt and fresh ground pepper

1 large egg

⅓ cup milk

1 medium onion, finely chopped

⅔ cup plain dried breadcrumbs

½ cup finely grated Parmesan cheese, plus more for serving

½ cup chopped fresh flat-leaf parsley

1 pound ground turkey (preferably 93 percent lean)

1 pound spaghetti

1 Make the sauce: In a large nonstick skillet, heat the oil over medium-high heat. Add the garlic, and cook for about 1 minute. Stir in the tomatoes, oregano, and thyme, and season with salt and pepper. Bring to a boil, lower the heat, and simmer, covered, for 20 to 25 minutes.

2 Meanwhile, make the meatballs: In a large bowl, whisk together the egg, milk, 1¼ teaspoons salt, and ¼ teaspoon pepper with a fork. Stir in the onion, breadcrumbs, cheese, and parsley. Add the turkey, and mix until combined. Form the mixture into 1½-inch balls.

3 Add the meatballs to the skillet, and spoon the sauce over to coat. Simmer over medium heat until the meatballs are just cooked through, about 8 minutes.

4 While the meatballs simmer, cook the spaghetti in a large pot of boiling salted water until al dente according to the package instructions. Drain the pasta, transfer to the skillet, and toss gently with the meatballs and sauce. Serve with more cheese.

FORMING MEATBALLS
Keeping your hands wet when shaping meatballs will prevent the meat from sticking, making the task much easier.

PREP TIME | **50** MINUTES

POTATO-CARROT PANCAKES

¾ pound (about 3 medium) white potatoes, peeled

8 ounces (about 3 medium) carrots, peeled

½ cup thinly sliced scallions (about 3 scallions)

Coarse salt

1 large egg, lightly beaten

¼ cup matzo meal

¼ cup vegetable oil, for frying

¼ cup reduced-fat sour cream, for serving (optional)

1 In a food processor fitted with a fine-hole grating attachment (or on the small holes of a box grater), grate the potatoes and carrots. Transfer to a large bowl; add the scallions and 1½ teaspoons salt. Using your hands, mix thoroughly. Mix in the egg and matzo meal until combined. Divide into 8 mounds of equal size.

2 In a large nonstick skillet, heat oil over medium-high heat, swirling to coat bottom of pan. Add half the potato mounds; flatten each to a ½-inch thickness. Cook until golden brown, 2 to 4 minutes per side.

3 Transfer to paper towels or parchment paper to drain. Repeat with the remaining mounds (reduce the temperature to medium if browning too quickly). Sprinkle with salt, and serve with the sour cream, if desired. **SERVES 4**

ROASTED PLUM TOMATOES

8 plum tomatoes (about 1½ pounds), cored and halved lengthwise

1 tablespoon olive oil

¼ teaspoon dried thyme

Coarse salt and fresh ground pepper

1 Preheat the oven to 425°F. Transfer the tomatoes to a rimmed baking sheet; toss with the olive oil, thyme, ½ teaspoon coarse salt, and ¼ teaspoon ground pepper until coated.

2 Arrange in a single layer, cut sides up. Bake until soft, about 30 minutes. **SERVES 4**

TOSSED RADICCHIO AND ENDIVE

2 tablespoons red-wine vinegar

2 tablespoons olive oil

1 tablespoon honey

Coarse salt and fresh ground pepper

1 medium radicchio (8 to 10 ounces), halved, cored, and thinly sliced lengthwise

2 medium Belgian endives (4 to 5 ounces each), ends trimmed, halved crosswise and thinly sliced lengthwise

In a large bowl, whisk together the vinegar, oil, and honey; season with salt and pepper. Add the radicchio and endives, and toss to coat. **SERVES 4**

GREEN BEANS WITH CARAMELIZED SHALLOTS

3 tablespoons butter

6 shallots, peeled and thinly sliced into rings

Coarse salt and fresh ground pepper

1 pound green beans, trimmed

1 In a medium saucepan with a tight-fitting lid, melt 2 tablespoons of the butter over medium heat; swirl to coat the bottom of the pan. Add the shallots; cover. Reduce the heat to medium-low; cook, stirring occasionally, until golden brown, 15 to 20 minutes. Set aside.

2 Meanwhile, in a large pot of boiling salted water, cook the green beans until fork-tender, 4 to 6 minutes. Drain; return to the pot. Toss with the remaining tablespoon butter. Season with salt and pepper.

3 Transfer the green beans to a serving dish; top with the caramelized shallots. **SERVES 4**

BABY BROCCOLI WITH ORANGE SAUCE

Coarse salt
2 bunches baby broccoli (about 1 pound), untrimmed
½ cup fresh orange juice
2 shallots, peeled, halved lengthwise, and thinly sliced
1 teaspoon balsamic vinegar
¼ teaspoon red pepper flakes (optional)

1 In a large pot of boiling salted water, cook the baby broccoli until just tender, 12 to 15 minutes; drain. Transfer to a serving bowl.

2 Meanwhile, in a small skillet, combine the orange juice, shallots, vinegar, and pepper flakes, if using; simmer over medium heat until reduced to ¼ cup, 3 to 4 minutes. Spoon the sauce over the baby broccoli; toss gently. **SERVES 4**

BUTTERNUT SQUASH WITH SAGE

2 tablespoons butter
2 pounds butternut squash, peeled, seeded, and cut into ¾-inch pieces
Coarse salt and fresh ground pepper
1 tablespoon chopped fresh sage (or ½ teaspoon dried)

1 Melt the butter in a 12-inch skillet over medium heat. Add the squash; season with salt and pepper. Cook, tossing frequently, until the squash is lightly browned, 5 to 6 minutes.

2 Add ¼ cup water and reduce the heat to a simmer. Cover, and cook until the squash is fork-tender, 8 to 10 minutes.

3 Toss with the sage. **SERVES 4**

GLAZED PEARL ONIONS

2 teaspoons olive oil
1 pound frozen pearl onions, thawed and patted dry
2 teaspoons sugar
Coarse salt and fresh ground pepper
1½ teaspoons fresh thyme (or ¼ teaspoon dried)

1 Heat the oil in a 10-inch skillet over medium heat. Add the onions. Cook, tossing occasionally, until beginning to brown, about 5 minutes.

2 Sprinkle with the sugar; season with salt and pepper. Add ⅔ cup water and the thyme; cook, stirring occasionally, until the onions are tender and the liquid has evaporated, about 20 minutes. **SERVES 4**

ROASTED CAULIFLOWER

1 head cauliflower (about 2 pounds), trimmed and cut into small florets
1 tablespoon olive oil
Coarse salt and fresh ground pepper
1 tablespoon butter
2 garlic cloves, thinly sliced
1 teaspoon capers
1 teaspoon caper juice

1 Preheat the oven to 450°F. Spread the cauliflower in a roasting pan. Drizzle with the oil; season with salt and pepper. Toss to combine. Roast, tossing once or twice, until the cauliflower is golden brown and tender, 20 to 25 minutes.

2 In a small skillet, melt the butter over medium heat. Cook the garlic, stirring often, until lightly browned, 2 to 3 minutes. Remove from heat. Add the capers and caper juice. Pour over the cauliflower, and toss to coat. **SERVES 4**

The topic for this cake is simple: cranberries are placed over sugar and spices at the bottom of the pan. As the cake bakes, the sugar caramelizes, forming a syrup. When you invert the pan, the syrup soaks into the cake, creating a festive dessert.

CRANBERRY UPSIDE-DOWN CAKE

SERVES 8 ■ PREP TIME: 20 MINUTES ■ **TOTAL TIME: 1 HOUR**

8 tablespoons unsalted butter, at room temperature

1 cup sugar

½ teaspoon ground cinnamon

¼ teaspoon ground allspice

1¾ cups cranberries

1 large egg

1 teaspoon vanilla extract

1¼ cups all-purpose flour

1½ teaspoons baking powder

¼ teaspoon salt

½ cup milk

Sweetened whipped cream, for serving (page 363, optional)

1 Preheat the oven to 350°F, with a rack in center. Rub the bottom and sides of an 8-inch round cake pan with 2 tablespoons of the butter. In a small bowl, whisk together ½ cup of the sugar with the cinnamon and allspice. Sprinkle the mixture evenly over the bottom of the pan; arrange the cranberries in a single layer on top.

2 With an electric mixer, cream the remaining 6 tablespoons butter and ½ cup sugar until light and fluffy. Add the egg and vanilla; beat until well combined. In another bowl, whisk together the flour, baking powder, and salt. With the mixer on low speed, add the flour mixture to the butter mixture in three batches, alternating with the milk, until well combined.

3 Spoon the batter over the cranberries in the pan, and smooth the top. Place the pan on a baking sheet; bake the cake until a toothpick inserted in the center comes out clean, 30 to 35 minutes. Let cool on a wire rack for 20 minutes. Run a knife around the edge of the cake; invert onto a rimmed platter. Serve with whipped cream on the side, if desired.

For a dinner party, you can present these cakes on a cake stand garnished with fresh berries.

GLAZED LEMON CAKES

MAKES 6 ■ PREP TIME: 15 MINUTES ■ **TOTAL TIME: 50 MINUTES**

½ cup (1 stick) unsalted butter, at room temperature, plus more for muffin tin

1½ cups all-purpose flour, plus more for muffin tin

2 teaspoons baking powder

½ teaspoon salt

½ cup low-fat buttermilk or plain low-fat yogurt

1 teaspoon vanilla extract

Finely grated zest and juice of 1 lemon, plus 2 tablespoons juice for the glaze

1 cup granulated sugar

2 large eggs

1½ cups confectioners' sugar

1 Preheat the oven to 350°F. Butter and flour a 6-cup jumbo muffin tin. In a medium bowl, whisk the flour with the baking powder and salt. In a small bowl, whisk together the buttermilk, vanilla, and lemon zest and juice. Set aside.

2 With an electric mixer, cream the butter and granulated sugar until light. Add the eggs one at a time, beating well after each addition. With the mixer on low speed, add the flour mixture in three batches, alternating with two additions of the buttermilk mixture.

3 Divide evenly among the muffin cups. Bake until a toothpick inserted in the center of a cake comes out clean, 20 to 25 minutes. Cool for 10 minutes in tin, then cool completely on a wire rack.

4 Set the rack over wax or parchment paper. In a small bowl, stir confectioners' sugar with the remaining 2 tablespoons lemon juice until smooth. Pour over the cakes, spreading to the edges with a small knife. Let set for 30 minutes before serving.

BUTTERING MUFFIN TINS
A pastry brush is great for coating muffin tins and other small baking pans with butter because it can reach into tight spots.

Serve this moist, molasses-rich gingerbread with whipped cream or vanilla ice cream. Drizzle the chocolate in a zigzag pattern over the batter, then drag a knife through the lines of chocolate, alternating the direction each time.

CHOCOLATE-SWIRL GINGERBREAD

MAKES 1 8-INCH CAKE ■ PREP TIME: 15 MINUTES ■ TOTAL TIME: 45 MINUTES

½ cup (1 stick) unsalted butter, plus more for pan

1½ cups all-purpose flour

½ cup packed light brown sugar

1½ teaspoons ground ginger

1 teaspoon baking powder

¼ teaspoon salt

⅛ teaspoon fresh ground pepper

⅛ teaspoon ground cloves

½ cup molasses

1 large egg, lightly beaten

2 ounces bittersweet chocolate, melted and slightly cooled

1 Preheat the oven to 325°F. Butter an 8-inch square pan. In a bowl, combine the flour, brown sugar, ginger, baking powder, salt, pepper, and cloves.

2 Melt the butter in ½ cup water in a small saucepan over medium heat, and stir the mixture into the dry ingredients until smooth. Stir in the molasses and lightly beaten egg.

3 Pour half the batter into the prepared pan. With a spoon, drizzle half the chocolate over the batter. Pour the remaining batter on top, and drizzle the remaining chocolate over the batter in a decorative pattern.

4 Bake the cake until a toothpick inserted in the center comes out clean, about 30 minutes. Cool completely on a wire rack.

DRIZZLING THE CHOCOLATE
Using a squeeze bottle is an easy way to drizzle chocolate over cake batter.

PREP TIME | **20** MINUTES

This no-fuss dessert lives up to its name—there's no cooking involved other than boiling water.

EASY TIRAMISÙ

SERVES 6 ■ PREP TIME: 20 MINUTES ■ **TOTAL TIME: 20 MINUTES**

3 tablespoons instant espresso powder

3 tablespoons boiling water

1 package (8 ounces) reduced-fat cream cheese

¾ cup heavy cream

⅓ cup sugar

2 packages (3 ounces each) soft ladyfingers

Unsweetened cocoa powder, for dusting

1 In a medium heat-proof bowl, mix the espresso powder with the boiling water until dissolved. Add 1½ cups cold water; set aside.

2 With an electric mixer, beat the cream cheese with the heavy cream and sugar until light and fluffy.

3 Spread a few tablespoons of the cream-cheese mixture in the bottom of a 2-quart serving dish. Separate the ladyfingers. One by one, dip a third of the ladyfingers in the espresso, then arrange in the bottom of the serving dish. Spread with a third of the cream-cheese mixture. Repeat twice with the remaining ladyfingers, espresso, and cream-cheese mixture. The tiramisù can be refrigerated, covered, for up to 1 day.

4 Dust with cocoa just before serving.

The easiest way to core a pineapple is to quarter it and then slice off the tip of each wedge, as illustrated below.

CARAMELIZED PINEAPPLE

SERVES 4 ■ PREP TIME: 20 MINUTES ■ TOTAL TIME: 20 MINUTES

2 tablespoons butter

1 pineapple, cored, peeled, and sliced lengthwise into eighths

½ cup sugar

Frozen yogurt, for serving (optional)

1 Heat the butter in a large nonstick skillet over high heat. Coat the pineapple wedges with the sugar; place in the hot pan. Cook, turning once and shaking the pan often, until golden brown, 8 to 10 minutes. Remove the pineapple.

2 Stir 3 tablespoons water into the pan, and heat briefly; drizzle over the pineapple. Serve with frozen yogurt, if desired.

PREP TIME | **20** MINUTES

You can prepare the batter through step two up to two hours ahead, then cover and refrigerate. Before baking, uncover and bring the batter to room temperature.

MOLTEN CHOCOLATE CAKES

SERVES 4 ■ PREP TIME: 15 MINUTES ■ **TOTAL TIME: 35 MINUTES**

4 tablespoons unsalted butter, at room temperature, plus more for muffin tins

⅓ cup granulated sugar, plus more for muffin tins

3 large eggs

⅓ cup all-purpose flour

¼ teaspoon salt

8 ounces bittersweet chocolate, melted

Confectioners' sugar, for dusting

Whipped cream, for serving (page 363; optional)

1 Preheat the oven to 400°F. Generously butter 4 cups of a standard muffin tin. Dust with granulated sugar, and tap out excess. Set aside.

2 In the bowl of an electric mixer, cream the butter and granulated sugar until fluffy. Add the eggs one at a time, beating well after each addition. With the mixer on low speed, beat in the flour and salt until just combined. Beat in the chocolate (do not overmix). Divide the batter evenly among the prepared muffin cups.

3 Place the muffin tin on a baking sheet; bake just until the tops of the cakes no longer jiggle when the pan is lightly shaken, 8 to 10 minutes. Remove from the oven; let stand for 10 minutes.

4 To serve, turn out the cakes, and place on serving plates, top sides up. Dust with confectioners' sugar, and serve with whipped cream, if desired.

MELTING CHOCOLATE
Place finely chopped chocolate in a heat-proof bowl set over a pan of gently simmering water; stir until just melted.

BASICS

CONSIDER THE RECIPES in this chapter the building blocks of the quick kitchen. If you can whip up a perfect batch of rice or polenta, you'll be better equipped to put a well-balanced meal on the table. Master the techniques for the recipes that follow, and you'll be on your way to practicing and enjoying the art of everyday cooking.

Vinaigrette is usually considered a salad dressing, but it also makes a fine sauce for vegetables, such as steamed green beans and boiled potatoes, and main dishes, such as broiled chicken or fish.

MARTHA'S FAVORITE VINAIGRETTE

MAKES 1 CUP ■ PREP TIME: 5 MINUTES ■ **TOTAL TIME: 5 MINUTES**

¼ cup white-wine vinegar
1 tablespoon Dijon mustard
Coarse salt and
fresh ground pepper
Pinch of sugar
¾ cup extra-virgin olive oil

1 In a small bowl, whisk together the vinegar, mustard, ¼ teaspoon salt, ⅛ teaspoon pepper, and the sugar.

2 Slowly add the oil, whisking until emulsified. Or shake the ingredients in a jar, or whirl them in a blender. Store in an airtight container or jar, and refrigerate for up to 2 weeks. Shake before using.

VARIATIONS

GARLIC

Add 1 teaspoon minced garlic or ½ clove, crushed.

SCALLION

Add 3 chopped whole scallions (about ¼ cup).

BALSAMIC

Substitute balsamic vinegar for the wine vinegar.

BLUE CHEESE

Add ½ cup crumbled blue cheese, such as Roquefort.

LEMON-PARMESAN

Use fresh lemon juice instead of vinegar; add ¼ cup finely grated Parmesan.

HERB

Add 2 tablespoons chopped fresh herbs, such as thyme, parsley, or tarragon.

FOOLPROOF HARD-COOKED EGGS

SERVES 4 ■ PREP TIME: 5 MINUTES ■ **TOTAL TIME: 15 MINUTES**

1 Place 4 eggs in a saucepan, and add enough water to cover them by 1 inch. Bring the water to a simmer over high heat. Remove from the heat, cover, and let stand for 12 minutes.

2 Drain and rinse under cold running water. Unpeeled eggs can be kept in the refrigerator for up to 1 week.

UNDERCOOKED
If you cut open an undercooked egg, the yolk will still be damp and will be a dark-gold color instead of pale yellow.

PERFECTLY COOKED
The white of a hard-cooked egg should be tender, the yolk fluffy but firm.

OVERCOOKED
The white of an overcooked egg is rubbery; the yolk develops an unattractive (though harmless) greenish-gray coating.

These are great basic techniques for chicken that you can use in any recipe that calls for rotisserie chicken. The poached chicken recipe produces broth that you can use whenever canned stock is called for.

POACHED CHICKEN BREASTS AND CHICKEN BROTH

PREP TIME: 20 MINUTES ■ TOTAL TIME: 45 MINUTES

4½ to 5 pounds bone-in, skin-on chicken breast halves (about 6)
1 onion, cut into 8 wedges
2 carrots, quartered crosswise
2 celery stalks, quartered crosswise
2 dried bay leaves
3 garlic cloves
6 sprigs fresh parsley
3 sprigs fresh thyme or ¼ teaspoon dried

1 Combine all ingredients in a 5-quart pot with a tight-fitting lid. Cover with water by 2 inches. Bring to a boil; reduce to a simmer, and cover. Cook the chicken until no longer pink in the center and an instant-read thermometer inserted in the thickest part of the meat (avoiding bone) registers 160°F, about 15 minutes.

2 Transfer the chicken to a rimmed baking sheet; arrange in a single layer, and let cool. With a slotted spoon, remove and discard the vegetables. Strain the broth through a fine-mesh sieve lined with a damp paper towel. If the broth is more than 8 cups (2 quarts), return to the pot; reduce over medium-high heat until you have just 8 cups. Once cooled, refrigerate for up to 2 days, or freeze for up to 3 months.

3 When the chicken is cool enough to handle, remove and discard the skin and bones. Shred with forks or chop the chicken, as desired.

MAKES 8 CUPS (2 POUNDS) POACHED CHICKEN AND 8 CUPS BROTH

EASY ROASTED CHICKEN

PREP TIME: 10 MINUTES
TOTAL TIME: 1 HOUR

1 whole chicken (about 3½ pounds),
  rinsed and patted dry

2 tablespoons butter,
  at room temperature

  Coarse salt and
  fresh ground pepper

1 Preheat the oven to 425°F. Tie the chicken legs together with kitchen twine (tuck the wings under the chicken, if desired, for a neater presentation). Place the chicken on a rack set in a roasting pan (or on a rimmed baking sheet).

2 Rub the chicken all over with the butter; season with 1 teaspoon salt and ½ teaspoon pepper. Roast until an instant-read thermometer registers 160°F when inserted in the thickest part of a thigh (avoiding bone), 45 to 50 minutes. Serve, or let cool before refrigerating, up to 3 days, covered.

BASICS: **RUBS**

MAKING RUBS

Almost any herbs or spices that are frequently combined, such as those in Italian seasonings or curry mixtures, can be made into a rub. Just add some salt (and sometimes sugar) to heighten the flavor.

HOW TO USE

Rubs should coat foods lightly. Use your fingers to rub the mixture on the meat, using about one teaspoon for every three quarters of a pound. Unlike most marinades, which often require soaking overnight, rubs can be applied just before cooking or up to several hours ahead.

CHILE RUB

- 1 tablespoon plus 1 teaspoon chili powder
- 2 teaspoons ground cumin
- 2 teaspoons brown sugar
- 1 teaspoon dried oregano
- 1 teaspoon coarse salt

In a small bowl, mix all ingredients. The brown sugar will caramelize slightly when cooked, giving foods a sweet, tasty glaze. Try it on whole chicken or turkey, pork (tenderloin or chops), and most cuts of beef.
MAKES 10 TEASPOONS

SPICY PAPRIKA RUB

- 4 teaspoons paprika
- 2 teaspoons coarse salt
- 1 teaspoon ground ginger
- 1 teaspoon ground cinnamon
- ½ teaspoon cayenne pepper
- ½ teaspoon ground allspice

In a small bowl, mix all ingredients. Because of paprika's strong taste, this rub is best paired with fattier foods, including salmon, skirt steak, pork loin, and whole chicken.
MAKES 9 TEASPOONS

THE RIGHT RUB

Which rub to use depends on the food you're preparing. The heartier the food, the stronger the rub should be. A piquant rub made with paprika and other spices is a good match for rich-tasting salmon. Chicken breasts, on the other hand, go better with a milder herb mix.

HOW TO STORE

A jar with a tight-fitting lid is good for mixing and storing. Dry rubs will keep for up to six months in a cool, dark place, so you can double or triple the recipes if you like. Wet rubs, such as Lemon-Herb Rub, should be refrigerated and will keep up to a week. Make sure to label and date the containers.

LEMON-HERB RUB

- 1 tablespoon dried tarragon
- 1 tablespoon grated lemon zest
- 4 dried bay leaves, crumbled
- 3 garlic cloves, minced
- 1½ teaspoons coarse salt
- ¾ teaspoon ground pepper
- 3 teaspoons olive oil

In a small bowl, mix all ingredients. This zesty rub is ideal for leaner foods such as turkey or chicken breasts and flaky white fish (such as halibut, cod, or snapper).
MAKES 12 TEASPOONS

CURRY RUB

- 4 teaspoons curry powder
- 1½ teaspoons ground coriander
- 1½ teaspoons coarse salt
- 1 teaspoon ground ginger
- 1 teaspoon ground cumin
- ½ teaspoon ground pepper
- ½ teaspoon sugar

In a small bowl, mix all ingredients. Lamb would be a good choice for this Indian-style rub. Or try it on chicken and shrimp. **MAKES 10 TEASPOONS**

BASICS: **HERB SAUCES**

PESTO

SALSA VERDE

GREEN GODDESS
DRESSING

ASIAN CILANTRO SAUCE

Fresh herbs give these sauces bright flavors. Use them to top grilled meats or steamed vegetables. They also make fantastic sandwich spreads.

SALSA VERDE

½ cup chopped fresh parsley

½ cup extra-virgin olive oil

3 tablespoons capers or dill gherkins, rinsed and chopped

1 tablespoon fresh lemon juice

1 tablespoon fresh oregano, chopped

1 garlic clove, chopped

Coarse salt (optional)

1 In a small bowl, combine the parsley, olive oil, capers or dill gherkins, lemon juice, oregano, and garlic.

2 Stir the mixture until well blended; season with salt, if desired.
MAKES ⅔ CUP

ASIAN CILANTRO SAUCE

2 cups loosely packed fresh cilantro leaves

2 tablespoons canola oil

1 tablespoon soy sauce

1 tablespoon rice vinegar

½ teaspoon sesame oil

Pinch of red pepper flakes

In a blender, purée the cilantro leaves, canola oil, 2 tablespoons water, soy sauce, rice vinegar, sesame oil, and red pepper flakes until smooth.
MAKES ½ CUP

PESTO

½ cup pine nuts or walnuts

4 cups fresh basil or parsley leaves, loosely packed

½ cup finely grated Parmesan cheese

1 garlic clove

Coarse salt and fresh ground pepper

½ cup extra-virgin olive oil

1 Preheat the oven to 350°F. Spread the pine nuts or walnuts on a rimmed baking sheet; toast in the oven until golden and fragrant, tossing occasionally, 5 to 8 minutes. Let cool completely.

2 In a food processor, combine the toasted nuts, basil or parsley leaves, Parmesan, and garlic; season with salt and pepper. Process until finely chopped. With the machine running, pour the olive oil in a steady stream through the feed tube; process until smooth. **MAKES 1¼ CUPS**

GREEN GODDESS DRESSING

1 cup mayonnaise

1 cup fresh parsley leaves

1 scallion, coarsely chopped

1 tablespoon fresh tarragon leaves

1 tablespoon white-wine vinegar

1 garlic clove

2 anchovy fillets or 1½ teaspoons anchovy paste (optional)

In a food processor, combine the mayonnaise, parsley, scallion, tarragon, vinegar, garlic, and anchovy fillets or anchovy paste. Process until the mixture is smooth and creamy.
MAKES 1¼ CUPS

BASICS: EASY CHUNKY TOMATO SAUCE

MAKES 6 CUPS
PREP TIME: 15 MINUTES
TOTAL TIME: 45 MINUTES

- 3 tablespoons olive oil
- 1 large onion, chopped (3 cups)
- 3 garlic cloves, chopped (about 1 tablespoon)
- Coarse salt and fresh ground pepper
- 2 cans (28 ounces each) diced tomatoes
- ½ teaspoon dried thyme or Italian seasoning

1 Heat the oil in a large saucepan over medium heat. Add the onion, garlic, ½ teaspoon salt, and ¼ teaspoon pepper, and cook until softened, about 5 minutes.

2 Add the tomatoes with their juice and the thyme; simmer, stirring occasionally, until the sauce has thickened, 20 to 25 minutes. The sauce can be frozen for up to 2 months.

BASICS: **HOW TO COOK PASTA**

GETTING STARTED
For each pound of pasta, you need at least four quarts of water. Use a six-quart (or larger) pot so that you have plenty of room for both and don't have to worry about the water boiling over. Add at least two tablespoons of coarse salt after the water comes to a boil.

PREVENTING STICKING
Enough water and frequent stirring are the keys to keeping pasta from sticking. You do not need to add oil to the water (this actually prevents sauces from clinging to the pasta). After adding the pasta, keep the heat on high, so the water returns to a boil as quickly as possible. Always cook uncovered.

WHEN IT'S DONE
Pasta should be al dente (firm to the bite). If undercooked, it will have a chalky core and floury taste; if over-cooked, it will be limp and soggy. Start tasting the pasta two to three minutes before the end of the suggested cooking time; pasta will continue to cook a bit after it's drained.

DRAINING
Before draining the pasta, reserve one to two cups of the cooking water; the water contains starch from the pasta that will add body to sauces. After pouring the pasta into a colander, shake it a few times but don't rinse it (unless you are making pasta salad).

FINISHING TOUCH
Immediately toss the pasta with the sauce of your choice, adding some reserved pasta water as needed to enhance the consistency of your dish.

BASICS: **PERFECT WHITE RICE**

SERVES 4
PREP TIME: 5 MINUTES
TOTAL TIME: 35 MINUTES

1 teaspoon salt
1 cup white rice (unconverted)

COOKING OTHER RICES
This recipe can be used to make basmati rice, too. To cook brown rice, increase the amount of water to 2¼ cups and the cooking time to 30 to 40 minutes; check rice after 30 minutes.

1 Bring 1¾ cups water and the salt to a rapid boil in a saucepan. Stir the rice into the boiling water.

2 Return the mixture to a boil; reduce heat to a simmer. Cover; cook without lifting the lid to prevent the steam from escaping until the rice is done (15 to 20 minutes; check toward the end of the cooking time).

3 The rice should be studded with steam holes when it is done.

4 Let stand, covered, for 5 to 10 minutes, then fluff the rice with a fork.

BASICS: **BEST COUSCOUS**

SERVES 4
PREP TIME: 5 MINUTES
TOTAL TIME: 20 MINUTES

2 cups couscous
(about 12 ounces)
Coarse salt and
fresh ground pepper
2 tablespoons olive oil
2½ cups boiling water

1 Put the couscous, ½ teaspoon salt, and ⅛ teaspoon pepper in a large bowl. Add the olive oil, and stir with a fork to coat evenly.

2 Stir one third of the boiling water into the couscous. Cover the remaining water to keep it hot.

3 Press the couscous gently with the back of the fork. Cover with plastic wrap; let stand for 3 minutes. Repeat with the remaining water in two additions.

4 Break up any clumps with a fork or your fingers.

BASICS: **SOFT POLENTA**

SERVES 4
PREP TIME: 20 MINUTES
TOTAL TIME: 20 MINUTES

Coarse salt and
fresh ground pepper
¾ cup yellow cornmeal or polenta
(not quick-cooking)
¼ cup finely grated cheese (Parmesan, Asiago, or sharp Cheddar)
1 tablespoon butter

1 In a large saucepan, bring 4 cups
water, 1½ teaspoons salt, and ⅛ teaspoon pepper to a boil over high
heat. Whisking constantly, very gradually add the cornmeal in a thin
stream, whisking until smooth before
adding more.

2 Reduce the heat to medium-low;
simmer, whisking often, until thickened, 10 to 15 minutes. Remove from
the heat; stir in the cheese and butter
until smooth. Serve immediately.

BASICS: **HOW TO COOK RISOTTO**

SERVES 6
PREP TIME: 10 MINUTES
TOTAL TIME: 45 MINUTES

   3 tablespoons olive oil
   1 small onion, finely chopped
1½ cups Arborio rice
   ¾ cup dry white wine
      Coarse salt and
      fresh ground pepper
4½ cups reduced-sodium
      canned chicken broth
   ¾ cup grated Parmesan cheese
   2 tablespoons butter
      Fresh thyme leaves,
      for garnish (optional)

1 In a medium saucepan, heat the oil over medium heat. Sauté the onion until tender, about 5 minutes. Add the rice; cook, stirring until well coated, 1 to 2 minutes. Add the wine; cook, stirring until absorbed, about 1 minute. Season with salt. Gently heat the broth; keep warm.

2 Add about 1 cup of the warm broth. Cook, stirring frequently, until absorbed. Continue adding broth, 1 cup at a time, stirring until most of the liquid has been absorbed, about 25 minutes total. The rice should be tender (but not mushy) and suspended in liquid with the consistency of heavy cream.

3 Remove the pan from the heat. Stir in the Parmesan and butter; season with salt and pepper. Serve immediately (risotto will continue to thicken as it sits). Garnish with thyme leaves, if desired.

BASICS: CHOCOLATE SAUCE

MAKES 1½ CUPS
PREP TIME: 5 MINUTES
TOTAL TIME: 5 MINUTES

¼ cup light corn syrup

6 ounces semisweet chocolate,
    broken or cut into small pieces

¾ cup heavy cream

1 In a small saucepan, combine the corn syrup and chocolate. Stir over medium-low heat until smooth, 4 to 5 minutes. Remove from the heat.

2 Whisk in the heavy cream until smooth. Serve right away, or let cool to room temperature before transferring to an airtight container. (The sauce can be refrigerated for up to 3 weeks. To serve, warm over low heat or in the microwave.)

BASICS: **WHIPPED CREAM**

MAKES ABOUT 2 CUPS
PREP TIME: 5 MINUTES
TOTAL TIME: 5 MINUTES

1 cup heavy cream
1 to 2 tablespoons granulated
  sugar

1 In a deep mixing bowl, beat the cream until soft peaks form.

2 Sprinkle the sugar over the cream; beat until soft peaks return. Do not overbeat.

HELPFUL HINTS
Make sure the cream is very cold; if you have time, chill the whisk (or beaters) and bowl in the freezer for about fifteen minutes. This will help the cream whip quickly and increase its volume.

ADDING FLAVOR
If you plan to use any flavoring, such as extracts, liqueurs, or spices, add them with the sugar in step two.

CHOICE OF TOOLS
A large hand-held whisk is very easy to use. If you are using an electric mixer, beat on medium speed, being careful not to overbeat (the cream will turn buttery). To use an immersion blender, whip the cream in a large liquid measuring cup (or other deep, narrow container) instead of a bowl; to avoid spattering, keep the blade submerged.

MAKING AHEAD
Whipped cream can be refrigerated, covered, for up to two hours before serving.

NUTRITIONAL INFORMATION

ALMOND-APRICOT CHICKEN WITH MINT PESTO 43

PER SERVING: 709 calories; 47.7 grams fat; 50.9 grams protein; 19.8 grams carbohydrates; 7.6 grams fiber

APPLE, ENDIVE, AND GRAPE SALAD 190

PER SERVING: 163 calories; 8.2 grams fat; 3.6 grams protein; 22.6 grams carbohydrates; 6 grams fiber

ARUGULA, BEET, AND GOAT-CHEESE SALAD 197

PER SERVING: 376 calories; 32.4 grams fat; 13.2 grams protein; 12.6 grams carbohydrates; 2.7 grams fiber

ASPARAGUS GRUYÈRE TART 69

PER SERVING: 558 calories; 39.6 grams fat; 20.2 grams protein; 32.8 grams carbohydrates; 2.3 grams fiber

BABY BROCCOLI WITH ORANGE SAUCE 331

PER SERVING: 71 calories; 0.1 grams fat; 4.7 grams protein; 13.8 grams carbohydrates; 1.4 grams fiber

BAKED RAVIOLI 313

PER SERVING: 647 calories; 26 grams fat; 30.7 grams protein; 73.2 grams carbohydrates; 6 grams fiber

BAKED SHELLS WITH WINTER SQUASH 322

PER SERVING: 534 calories; 15.4 grams fat; 18.5 grams protein; 80.9 grams carbohydrates; 6.1 grams fiber

BARBECUED CHICKEN 112

PER SERVING: 626 calories; 26.7 grams fat; 45.5 grams protein; 52.3 grams carbohydrates; 0.6 gram fiber

BEEF AND ORANGE STIR-FRY 212

PER SERVING: 495 calories; 16.8 grams fat; 32.3 grams protein; 54 grams carbohydrates; 4.2 grams fiber

BEEF BULGOGI 215

PER SERVING: 552 calories; 37.9 grams fat; 35.1 grams protein; 17.7 grams carbohydrates; 2.1 grams fiber

BEEF TACOS WITH RADISH AND AVOCADO SALSA 49

PER SERVING: 437 calories; 24.5 grams fat; 26.9 grams protein; 28.4 grams carbohydrates; 7 grams fiber

BEST BEEF BURGERS 127

PER SERVING: 446 calories; 29.7 grams fat; 40 grams protein; 1 gram carbohydrates; 0.1 gram fiber

BEST COUSCOUS 359

PER SERVING: 313 calories; 2.8 grams fat; 9.9 grams protein; 60.4 grams carbohydrates; 2.5 grams fiber

BEST POLENTA 360

PER SERVING: 142 calories; 4.7 grams fat; 4.2 grams protein; 20.4 grams carbohydrates; 1.9 grams fiber

BLACKBERRY AND GINGER TRIFLE 176

PER SERVING: 461 calories; 29.4 grams fat; 4.7 grams protein; 47 grams carbohydrates; 2.8 grams fiber

BLUEBERRY CRUMB CAKE 180

PER SERVING: 405 calories; 16.7 grams fat; 5.2 grams protein; 59.7 grams carbohydrates; 1.7 grams fiber

BOK CHOY, CARROT, AND APPLE SLAW 171

PER SERVING: 82 calories; 3.9 grams fat; 2.2 grams protein; 11.9 grams carbohydrates; 2.9 grams fiber

BRAISED CHICKEN WITH MUSHROOMS AND OVEN-BAKED POLENTA 201

PER SERVING: 294 calories; 10 grams fat; 43 grams protein; 7 grams carbohydrates; 1.6 grams fiber

BROCCOLI, CHICKPEA, AND TOMATO SALAD 194

PER SERVING: 131 calories; 5.9 grams fat; 5.5 grams protein; 15.8 grams carbohydrates; 4.9 grams fiber

BRUSSELS SPROUTS AND HAZELNUTS 247

PER SERVING: 96 calories; 5.4 grams fat; 4.4 grams protein; 10.8 grams carbohydrates; 4.7 grams fiber

BUTTERMILK BAKED CHICKEN 35

PER SERVING: 703 calories; 37.6 grams fat; 6.9 grams protein; 17.9 grams carbohydrates; 0.7 gram fiber

BUTTERMILK MASHED POTATOES 247

PER SERVING: 183 calories; 6.2 grams fat; 4 grams protein; 28.2 grams carbohydrates; 2.9 grams fiber

BUTTERNUT SQUASH WITH SAGE 331

PER SERVING: 137 calories; 6 grams fat; 2 grams protein; 22.5 grams carbohydrates; 3.5 grams fiber

CANTALOUPE AND BOCCONCINI SALAD WITH MINT 107

PER SERVING: 264 calories; 16 grams fat; 16 grams protein; 14.3 grams carbohydrates; 1.6 grams fiber

CANTALOUPE WITH HONEY AND LIME 179

PER SERVING: 114 calories; 0.4 gram fat; 1.3 grams protein; 29.5 grams carbohydrates; 1.2 grams fiber

CAPPUCCINO PARFAITS 259

PER SERVING: 207 calories; 8.3 grams fat; 10.7 grams protein; 25.6 grams carbohydrates; 0 gram fiber

CARAMELIZED PINEAPPLE 340

PER SERVING (WITHOUT YOGURT): 255 calories; 6.7 grams fat; 1 gram protein; 52.4 grams carbohydrates

CARROT-CUMIN SLAW 35

PER SERVING: 160 calories; 13.9 grams fat; 1.3 grams protein; 9.2 grams carbohydrates; 3.1 grams fiber

CARROT CUPCAKES 94

PER SERVING: 307 calories; 17.3 grams fat; 4.3 grams protein; 35.1 grams carbohydrates; 1 gram fiber

CARROT SLAW WITH YOGURT DRESSING 232

PER SERVING: 67 calories; 0.9 grams fat; 3 grams protein; 13.7 grams carbohydrates; 3.8 grams fiber

CASHEW CHICKEN 40

PER SERVING: 477 calories; 22.5 grams fat; 49 grams protein; 21.1 grams carbohydrates; 1 gram fiber

CHERRY TOMATO CRISP 83

PER SERVING: 121 calories; 5.9 grams fat; 4.5 grams protein; 14.2 grams carbohydrates; 2.2 grams fiber

CHICKEN CAESAR SALAD 119

PER SERVING: 349 calories; 18.6 grams fat; 23.1 grams protein; 22 grams carbohydrates; 2.4 grams fiber

CHICKEN CHILAQUILES 44

PER SERVING: 484 calories; 19.9 grams fat; 46.3 grams protein; 27.7 grams carbohydrates; 1.8 grams fiber

CHICKEN CURRY 283

PER SERVING: 354 calories; 8.1 grams fat; 42.6 grams protein; 25.1 grams carbohydrates; 3.2 grams fiber

CHICKEN PARMIGIANA 39

PER SERVING: 729 calories; 37.6 grams fat; 60.2 grams protein; 36.2 grams carbohydrates; 0.9 gram fiber

CHICKEN STIR-FRY WRAPS 202

PER SERVING: 298 calories; 9.1 grams fat; 41.6 grams protein; 11.3 grams carbohydrates; 1.7 grams fiber

CHICKEN WITH CRANBERRY SAUCE 290

PER SERVING: 379 calories; 15.4 grams fat; 38.2 grams protein; 20.5 grams carbohydrates; 1.7 grams fiber

CHICKEN WITH POBLANO CREAM SAUCE 205

PER SERVING: 275 calories; 15.6 grams fat; 28.3 grams protein; 4.5 grams carbohydrates; 0.6 gram fiber

CHICKEN WITH PROSCIUTTO AND SAGE 276

PER SERVING: 393 calories; 12.7 grams fat; 52.8 grams protein; 7.1 grams carbohydrates; 0.6 gram fiber

CHILI-RUBBED SALMON WITH ZUCCHINI AND SAUTÉED CORN 149

PER SERVING: 377 calories; 15.3 grams fat; 38.6 grams protein; 24 grams carbohydrates; 4.7 grams fiber

CHILI-RUBBED SKIRT STEAKS 294

PER SERVING: 345 calories; 22.5 grams fat; 31.6 grams protein; 2.3 grams carbohydrates; 0.8 gram fiber

CHOCOLATE-SAUCE GRASSHOPPER SUNDAES 93

PER SERVING: 413 calories; 22.4 grams fat; 5.8 grams protein; 48.9 grams carbohydrates; 2 grams fiber

CHOCOLATE-SWIRL GINGERBREAD 336

PER SERVING: 435 calories; 18.9 grams fat; 4.8 grams protein; 63.8 grams carbohydrates; 1 gram fiber

COCONUT SHRIMP SOUP 186

PER SERVING: 538 calories;
22.7 grams fat; 41.4 grams protein;
43.8 grams carbohydrates;
3.7 grams fiber

**COD WITH FENNEL AND
POTATOES 305**

PER SERVING: 299 calories;
4.9 grams fat; 35.1 grams protein;
28.7 grams carbohydrates;
4.6 grams fiber

**COD WITH LEEKS AND
TOMATOES 61**

PER SERVING: 249 calories;
5.2 grams fat; 37 grams protein;
13.1 grams carbohydrates;
1.9 grams fiber

CORN AND RADISH SALAD 112

PER SERVING: 112 calories;
4.5 grams fat; 3 grams protein;
18.3 grams carbohydrates;
2.7 grams fiber

CORN FRITTERS 169

PER SERVING: 222 calories;
11 grams fat; 6.8 grams protein;
26.8 grams carbohydrates;
2.4 grams fiber

CORN SALAD 169

PER SERVING: 199 calories;
10.5 grams fat; 6.2 grams protein;
24.8 grams carbohydrates;
3.3 grams fiber

**CRANBERRY UPSIDE-DOWN
CAKE 332**

PER SERVING: 305 calories;
12.9 grams fat; 3.5 grams protein;
44.7 grams carbohydrates;
1.6 grams fiber

CREAM OF ASPARAGUS SOUP 17

PER SERVING: 139 calories;
8.2 grams fat; 5.1 grams protein;
14.6 grams carbohydrates;
3.9 grams fiber

CREAMY BROCCOLI SOUP 189

PER SERVING: 150 calories;
8.3 grams fat; 6.8 grams protein;
15.4 grams carbohydrates;
5.7 grams fiber

CREAMY CORN SOUP 99

PER SERVING: 216 calories;
8 grams fat; 6.3 grams protein;
36.6 grams carbohydrates;
5.2 grams fiber

**CREAMY FETTUCCINE WITH
ASPARAGUS 78**

PER SERVING: 496 calories;
13.3 grams fat; 24.5 grams protein;
75.1 grams carbohydrates;
7.7 grams fiber

CREAMY PARSNIP SOUP 264

PER SERVING: 349 calories;
17.6 grams fat; 6 grams protein;
44.8 grams carbohydrates;
9 grams fiber

CRISP GOAT-CHEESE SALAD 31

PER SERVING: 589 calories;
46.9 grams fat; 21.8 grams protein;
20.4 grams carbohydrates;
4.4 grams fiber

**CRISPY APRICOT PORK
CHOPS 296**

PER SERVING: 404 calories;
20.4 grams fat; 37.7 grams protein;
15.3 grams carbohydrates;
1 gram fiber

CUCUMBER-RADISH SLAW 83

PER SERVING: 56 calories;
2.6 grams fat; 1.4 grams protein;
7.3 grams carbohydrates;
1.7 grams fiber

CURRIED CARROT SOUP 267

PER SERVING: 185 calories;
6.3 grams fat; 5.7 grams protein;
28.3 grams carbohydrates;
7.8 grams fiber

CURRIED ZUCCHINI SOUP 100

PER SERVING: 164 calories;
0.9 gram fat; 5.4 grams protein;
21.4 grams carbohydrates;
4.3 grams fiber

**EASY CHUNKY TOMATO
SAUCE 356**

PER 3/4 CUP SERVING: 106 calories;
5.6 grams fat; 2.5 grams protein;
13.4 grams carbohydrates;
2.4 grams fiber

EASY ROASTED CHICKEN 351

PER SERVING: 502 calories;
31.4 grams fat; 51.6 grams protein;
0.2 gram carbohydrates;
0.1 gram fiber

EASY TIRAMISÙ 339

PER SERVING: 348 calories;
22.5 grams fat; 7.4 grams protein;
30.1 grams carbohydrates;
0.4 gram fiber

**ENCHILADAS WITH
PUMPKIN SAUCE 279**

PER SERVING: 537 calories;
28 grams fat; 35.2 grams protein;
36.7 grams carbohydrates;
8.4 grams fiber

**FARFALLE WITH SALMON, MINT,
AND PEAS 81**

PER SERVING: 563 calories;
17.5 grams fat; 34.9 grams protein;
64.3 grams carbohydrates;
4 grams fiber

FAVORITE TURKEY BURGER 123

PER SERVING (WITHOUT BUNS):
290 calories; 9.7 grams fat;
37.6 grams protein;
7.1 grams carbohydrates;
0.9 gram fiber

**FENNEL, ORANGE, AND
PARSLEY SALAD 271**

PER SERVING: 131 calories;
2.2 grams fat; 2.6 grams protein;
28.9 grams carbohydrates;
7.7 grams fiber

FISH PO'BOYS 231

PER SERVING: 387 calories;
19 grams fat; 24.9 grams protein;
25.7 grams carbohydrates;
1.1 grams fiber

FISH TACOS 150

PER SERVING: 399 calories;
11.5 grams fat; 30.7 grams protein;
42.5 grams carbohydrates;
3.7 grams fiber

**FLANK STEAK
WITH LIME MARINADE 130**

PER SERVING: 296 calories;
14.2 grams fat; 37.1 grams protein;
3.6 grams carbohydrates;
0.3 gram fiber

FRESH TOMATO SALSA 154

PER 1/4 CUP SERVING: 12 calories;
0.1 grams fat; 0.5 grams protein;
2.6 grams carbohydrates;
0.7 gram fiber

**GARLIC-MARINATED CHICKEN
CUTLETS WITH
GRILLED POTATOES 116**

PER SERVING: 478 calories;
17.4 grams fat; 47.5 grams protein;
32 grams carbohydrates;
6.8 grams fiber

**GARLIC-ROASTED CHICKEN
BREASTS 275**

PER SERVING: 551 calories;
29.2 grams fat; 61.5 grams protein;
16.7 grams carbohydrates;
1.1 grams fiber

GINGERED SUGAR SNAPS 83

PER SERVING: 85 calories;
3.5 grams fat; 2.7 grams protein;
9.6 grams carbohydrates;
2.7 grams fiber

GLAZED CARROTS 85

PER SERVING: 128 calories;
6 grams fat; 1.6 grams protein;
18.5 grams carbohydrates

GLAZED LEMON CAKES 335

PER SERVING: 532 calories;
17.3 grams fat; 6.2 grams protein;
89.5 grams carbohydrates;
1 gram fiber

GLAZED PEARL ONIONS 331

PER SERVING: 69 calories;
2.3 grams fat; 1 gram protein;
11.7 grams carbohydrates;
2 grams fiber

**GLAZED PORK TENDERLOIN
WITH PINEAPPLE 223**

PER SERVING: 292 calories;
6.3 grams fat; 36.3 grams protein;
23.4 grams carbohydrates;
1.1 grams fiber

**GREEK SALAD WITH SEASONED
FLATBREAD 28**

PER SERVING: 389 calories;
31 grams fat; 12.2 grams protein;
18.2 grams carbohydrates;
4.2 grams fiber

**GREEK-STYLE MINI
LAMB BURGERS 142**

PER SERVING: 524 calories;
24.7 grams fat; 35.8 grams protein;
37.3 grams carbohydrates;
1.5 grams fiber

**GREEN BEANS WITH CARAMELIZED
SHALLOTS 329**

PER SERVING: 139 calories;
8.7 grams fat; 3.6 grams protein;
15.2 grams carbohydrates;
3.9 grams fiber

**GRILLED CHOCOLATE
SANDWICHES 255**

PER 1/2 SANDWICH SERVING:
350 calories; 19.9 grams fat;
9.3 grams protein; 36.5 grams
carbohydrates; 2.9 grams fiber

GRILLED CORN ON THE COB 166

PER SERVING: 115 calories;
5.3 grams fat; 4 grams protein;
16 grams carbohydrates;
2 grams fiber

**GRILLED PEACHES WITH
SWEETENED SOUR CREAM 175**

PER SERVING: 206 calories;
11.6 grams fat; 2.3 grams protein;
23.1 grams carbohydrates;
2 grams fiber

**GRILLED SWEET POTATOES WITH
SCALLIONS 171**

PER SERVING: 317 calories;
16.4 grams fat; 3 grams protein;
40.9 grams carbohydrates;
5.2 grams fiber

GRILLED TOMATO LINGUINE 162

PER SERVING (BASED ON 6):
467 calories; 16 grams fat;
15.4 grams protein; 66.6 grams
carbohydrates; 4.6 grams fiber

**GRILLED TUSCAN CHICKEN WITH
ROSEMARY AND LEMON 120**

PER SERVING: 575 calories;
39 grams fat; 51.3 gram protein;
2.1 grams carbohydrates;
0.2 grams fiber

**GRILLED VEGETABLE
TOSTADAS 154**

PER SERVING: 508 calories;
22.6 grams fat; 18.5 grams protein;
64.1 grams carbohydrates;
9.7 grams fiber

**GRILLED ZUCCHINI AND
SQUASH 120**

PER SERVING: 178 calories;
14.1 grams fat; 3.1 grams protein;
12.7 grams carbohydrates;
3.2 grams fiber

HERB-CRUSTED SNAPPER 146

PER SERVING (WITHOUT COUSCOUS): 238
calories; 6 grams fat;
40.9 grams protein; 0.4 gram
carbohydrates; 0.3 grams fiber

HOT AND SOUR SOUP 20

PER SERVING: 109 calories;
2.7 grams fat; 8.6 grams protein;
11.8 grams carbohydrates;
0.5 gram fiber

**ICEBERG WEDGES WITH
THOUSAND ISLAND DRESSING 268**

PER SERVING: 143 calories;
10.9 grams fat; 5.3 grams protein;
7.2 grams carbohydrates;
1.5 grams fiber

**INDIAN-SPICED
CHICKEN BURGERS 124**

PER SERVING (WITH CUMIN YOGURT
SAUCE): 423 calories;
9.5 grams fat; 42.6 grams protein;
43.8 grams carbohydrates;
6.7 grams fiber

JICAMA SLAW 171
PER SERVING: 47 calories;
0.1 gram fat; 0.9 gram protein;
11.2 grams carbohydrates;
5.7 grams fiber

**LAMB CHOPS WITH
MINT-PEPPER SAUCE 57**
PER SERVING: 258 calories;
14.2 grams fat; 28.2 grams protein;
2.7 grams carbohydrates;
1.1 grams fiber

**LAMB CHOPS WITH
YOGURT SAUCE 227**
PER SERVING: 419 calories;
31.5 grams fat; 29.6 grams protein;
2.8 grams carbohydrates;
0 gram fiber

**LEAF-LETTUCE SALAD WITH
PARMESAN CRISPS 27**
PER SERVING (WITH DRESSING): 107
calories; 9.3 grams fat; 3.7 grams
protein; 2.8 grams carbohydrates;
1.2 grams fiber

LEMON CUSTARD CAKES 90
PER SERVING: 161 calories;
5.8 grams fat; 4.8 grams protein;
23.1 grams carbohydrates;
0.2 gram fiber

**LEMON-GARLIC LAMB
KEBABS 141**
PER SERVING (WITH FETA DIPPING SAUCE):
373 calories;
25 grams fat; 33.2 grams protein;
2.6 grams carbohydrates;
0.1 gram fiber

**LEMON-PARSLEY PORK
CHOPS 299**
PER SERVING: 373 calories;
29 grams fat; 25.9 grams protein;
0.6 gram carbohydrates;
0.2 gram fiber

LEMON-THYME GREEN BEANS 293
PER SERVING: 106 calories;
5.9 grams fat; 3.2 grams protein;
13.2 gram carbohydrates;
5.9 grams fiber

LENTIL SOUP 263
PER SERVING: 346 calories;
4.3 grams fat; 26.1 grams protein;
54.1 grams carbohydrates;
24.7 grams fiber

LENTIL-WALNUT BURGERS 153
PER SERVING (WITHOUT YOGURT-
CILANTRO SAUCE): 460 calories;
28.9 grams fat; 18.7 grams protein;
35 grams carbohydrates;
13.6 grams fiber

**LINGUINE WITH SAUSAGE AND
PEPPERS 74**
PER SERVING: 498 calories;
16.3 grams fat; 23.6 grams protein;
63.5 grams carbohydrates;
3.1 grams fiber

MACARONI AND CHEESE 317
PER SERVING: 553 calories;
24.9 grams fat; 26.2 grams protein;
56.1 grams carbohydrates;
2.5 grams fiber

**MANGO AND HEARTS
OF PALM SALAD WITH LIME
VINAIGRETTE 272**
PER SERVING: 70 calories;
1.1 grams fat; 2.8 grams protein;
15.3 grams carbohydrates;
3.1 grams fiber

MASHED WHITE BEANS 290
PER SERVING: 223 calories;
4.9 grams fat; 14 grams protein;
30.8 grams carbohydrates;
10.8 grams fiber

**MEDITERRANEAN CHICKEN
STEW 287**
PER SERVING (WITH POLENTA):
464 calories; 12.6 grams fat;
47.4 grams protein;
38.4 grams carbohydrates;
5.5 grams fiber

**MIXED GREEN SALAD
WITH CITRUS DRESSING 54**
PER SERVING: 127 calories;
7.5 grams fat; 2.4 grams protein;
14.1 grams carbohydrates;
1.7 grams fiber

MIXED TOMATO SALAD 104
PER SERVING: 152 calories;
11.5 grams fat; 3.3 grams protein;
11.5 grams carbohydrates;
3.1 grams fiber

MOLTEN CHOCOLATE CAKES 342
PER SERVING: 568 calories;
37 grams fat; 9.8 grams protein;
60.4 grams carbohydrates;
1.6 grams fiber

**MOROCCAN CHICKEN
COUSCOUS 280**
PER SERVING: 735 calories;
13.1 grams fat; 58.8 grams protein;
93.4 grams carbohydrates;
10.1 grams fiber

**MUSHROOM RAGOUT WITH
PASTA 314**
PER SERVING: 290 calories;
3.1 grams fat; 12.8 grams protein;
52.5 grams carbohydrates;
2.4 grams fiber

MUSHROOM TART 306
PER SERVING: 219 calories;
12.7 grams fat; 7.8 grams protein;
21 grams carbohydrates;
4.6 grams fiber

**ORECCHIETTE WITH SAUSAGE AND
ROASTED PEPPERS 239**
PER SERVING: 459 calories;
12.3 grams fat; 25.1 grams protein;
63.1 grams carbohydrates;
3.5 grams fiber

ORZO AND SNAP PEA SALAD 227
PER SERVING: 218 calories;
5.7 grams fat; 7.7 grams protein;
36 grams carbohydrates;
4.5 grams fiber

**PAN-FRIED SHRIMP WITH GREEN
CURRY CASHEW SAUCE 62**
PER SERVING: 410 calories;
20.6 grams fat; 40.3 grams protein;
16.5 grams carbohydrates;
1.1 grams fiber

PARMESAN STEAK FRIES 83

PER SERVING: 272 calories;
7.4 grams fat; 16.4 grams protein;
35.8 grams carbohydrates;
2.5 grams fiber

PARMESAN-STUFFED CHICKEN BREASTS 206

PER SERVING: 429 calories;
6.1 grams fat; 81.9 grams protein;
6.3 grams carbohydrates;
1 gram fiber

PASTA AND EASY ITALIAN MEAT SAUCE 243

PER SERVING: 597 calories;
27.3 grams fat; 21.5 grams protein;
66.3 grams carbohydrates;
3.5 grams fiber

PASTA WITH LENTILS AND ARUGULA 318

PER SERVING: 397 calories;
7.8 grams fat; 18.9 grams protein;
64.9 grams carbohydrates;
11.1 grams fiber

PASTA WITH PESTO, POTATOES, AND GREEN BEANS 158

PER SERVING: 421 calories;
16 grams fat; 12.2 grams protein;
58.6 grams carbohydrates;
4.1 grams fiber

PASTA WITH PROSCIUTTO AND PEAS 161

PER SERVING: 639 calories;
25.5 grams fat; 27.8 grams protein;
76.8 grams carbohydrates;
5.9 grams fiber

PEAR CUSTARD PIE 256

PER SERVING: 263 calories;
12.3 grams fat; 5.3 grams protein;
33.9 grams carbohydrates;
2.7 grams fiber

PECAN-CRUSTED CATFISH 232

PER SERVING: 438 calories;
32 grams fat; 28.1 grams protein;
9.9 grams carbohydrates;
1.5 grams fiber

PERFECT WHITE RICE 358

PER SERVING: 169 calories;
0.3 gram fat; 3.3 grams protein;
37 grams carbohydrates;
0.5 gram fiber

PESTO 355

PER TABLESPOON SERVING:
158 calories; 15.8 grams fat;
1.8 grams protein;
3.5 grams carbohydrates;
2.7 grams fiber

POACHED CHICKEN BREASTS AND CHICKEN BROTH 350

PER SERVING: 147 calories;
3.1 grams fat; 26.9 grams protein;
1 grams carbohydrates;
0 gram fiber

PORK CHOPS WITH APPLES AND SHALLOTS 224

PER SERVING: 505 calories;
27.8 grams fat; 40.4 grams protein;
18.3 grams carbohydrates;
1.7 grams fiber

PORK CHOPS WITH RHUBARB-CHERRY SAUCE 53

PER SERVING: 587 calories;
33.2 grams fat; 41.7 grams protein;
27.9 grams carbohydrates;
2.9 grams fiber

PORK QUESADILLAS 138

PER SERVING: 654 calories;
29.2 grams fat; 48.5 grams protein;
46.2 grams carbohydrates;
3.5 grams fiber

PORK TENDERLOIN WITH MUSTARD SAUCE 54

PER SERVING: 206 calories;
8.6 grams fat; 28.9 grams protein;
2.5 grams carbohydrates;
0.5 gram fiber

POTATO AND ONION FRITTATA 309

PER SERVING: 238 calories;
13.2 grams fat; 14.2 grams protein;
15.6 grams carbohydrates;
1.6 grams fiber

POTATO-CARROT PANCAKES 329

PER SERVING: 245 calories;
15.5 grams fat; 4.4 grams protein;
24.3 grams carbohydrates;
4.2 grams fiber

POTATO-LEEK SOUP 23

PER SERVING: 310 calories;
17.5 grams fat; 8.1 grams protein;
32.8 grams carbohydrates;
3.4 grams fiber

POTATO SALAD WITH SOUR CREAM AND SCALLIONS 128

PER SERVING: 349 calories;
16.8 grams fat; 6.9 grams protein;
43.6 grams carbohydrates;
5.4 grams fiber

PURÉED BUTTERNUT SQUASH SOUP 185

PER SERVING: 185 calories;
6 grams fat; 3.1 grams protein;
34.5 grams carbohydrates;
9.3 grams fiber

RED CABBAGE WITH APPLE 220

PER SERVING (BASED ON 6): 95 calories;
4.8 grams fat; 2.6 grams protein;
12.6 grams carbohydrates;
3.1 grams fiber

RHUBARB CRISP 89

PER SERVING (WITHOUT ICE CREAM): 235
calories; 8.3 grams fat;
2.6 grams protein;
39 grams carbohydrates;
0.9 gram fiber

RIGATONI WITH GOAT CHEESE 165

PER SERVING: 452 calories;
14.9 grams fat; 21.2 grams protein;
57.8 grams carbohydrates;
1.8 grams fiber

RIGATONI WITH SAUSAGE AND PARSLEY 325

PER SERVING: 594 calories;
27 grams fat; 25.6 grams protein;
62.1 grams carbohydrates;
3.4 grams fiber

RISOTTO 361

PER SERVING: 261 calories; 13.8 grams fat; 8.5 grams protein; 20.7 grams carbohydrates; 0.4 gram fiber

ROAST BEEF WITH SHALLOTS AND NEW POTATOES 293

PER SERVING: 460 calories; 13.1 grams fat; 45.1 grams protein; 40.7 grams carbohydrates; 2.9 grams fiber

ROASTED ACORN SQUASH, SHALLOTS, AND ROSEMARY 247

PER SERVING: 146 calories; 6.9 grams fat; 2.2 grams protein; 22.1 grams carbohydrates; 2.3 grams fiber

ROASTED ASPARAGUS WITH PARMESAN 85

PER SERVING: 91 calories; 5.4 grams fat; 6.2 grams protein; 6.9 grams carbohydrates; 2.5 grams fiber

ROASTED CAULIFLOWER 331

PER SERVING: 79 calories; 6.4 grams fat; 1.9 grams protein; 4.9 grams carbohydrates; 2.2 grams fiber

ROASTED CHICKEN AND VEGETABLES 208

PER SERVING: 543 calories; 24.8 grams fat; 52.9 grams protein; 28.5 grams carbohydrates; 7 grams fiber

ROASTED CHICKEN BREASTS WITH CARROTS AND ONION 284

PER SERVING: 507 calories; 14.4 grams fat; 56.7 grams protein; 34.9 grams carbohydrates; 5.5 grams fiber

ROASTED CORNISH HENS WITH GRAPES 198

PER SERVING: 505 calories; 16.3 grams fat; 53.9 grams protein; 37.6 grams carbohydrates; 1.8 grams fiber

ROASTED FENNEL 247

PER SERVING: 65 calories; 3.6 grams fat; 1.4 grams protein; 8.3 grams carbohydrates; 3.5 grams fiber

ROASTED FRUIT 251

PER SERVING (WITHOUT ICE CREAM OR YOGURT): 154 calories; 6.2 grams fat; 1.3 grams protein; 25.9 grams carbohydrates; 2.6 grams fiber

ROASTED PEARS AND SWEET POTATOES 249

PER SERVING: 333 calories; 11.2 grams fat; 3.4 grams protein; 57.4 grams carbohydrates; 7.6 grams fiber

ROASTED PLUM TOMATOES 329

PER SERVING: 66 calories; 4 grams fat; 1.5 grams protein; 8 grams carbohydrates; 1.9 grams fiber

ROASTED PORK WITH BLACK-EYED PEA SALAD 137

PER SERVING (WITH BLACK-EYED PEA SALAD): 404 calories; 17.2 grams fat; 38.5 grams protein; 26.5 grams carbohydrates; 5.2 grams fiber

ROASTED SALMON WITH LEMON RELISH 58

PER SERVING: 439 calories; 26.8 grams fat; 36.2 grams protein; 14.6 grams carbohydrates; 2.7 grams fiber

ROASTED SALMON WITH LENTILS 228

PER SERVING: 484 calories; 22.7 grams fat; 44.4 grams protein; 23.6 grams carbohydrates; 4.9 grams fiber

ROMAINE HEART SALAD WITH CREAMY CHILI DRESSING 295

PER SERVING: 68 calories; 4.5 grams fat; 1.9 grams protein; 5.8 grams carbohydrates; 1.3 grams fiber

RUM-GLAZED SHRIMP AND MANGO 145

PER SERVING: 235 calories; 8.1 grams fat; 12.1 grams protein; 23.2 grams carbohydrates; 1.5 grams fiber

RUSTIC APPLE TART 252

PER SERVING: 374 calories; 20.4 grams fat; 3.7 grams protein; 45.7 grams carbohydrates; 2.1 grams fiber

RYE-CRUSTED PORK MEDALLIONS 220

PER SERVING: 481 calories; 30.4 grams fat; 37.8 grams protein; 11.7 grams carbohydrates; 1.5 grams fiber

SALMON NIÇOISE SALAD 66

PER SERVING (WITH DRESSING): 497 calories; 29.1 grams fat; 35.1 grams protein; 24.8 grams carbohydrates; 5.3 grams fiber

SALMON STEAKS WITH HOISIN GLAZE 301

PER SERVING: 312 calories; 16.4 grams fat; 30.1 grams protein; 7.8 grams carbohydrates; 0 gram fiber

SAUTÉED BOK CHOY AND BROCCOLI 249

PER SERVING (BASED ON 6): 65.2 calories; 4.8 grams fat; 2.6 grams protein; 4.5 grams carbohydrates; 2 grams fiber

SAUTÉED BROCCOLI RABE 275

PER SERVING: 96 calories; 6.6 grams fat; 5.5 grams protein; 7 grams carbohydrates; 0.3 gram fiber

SAUTÉED CHICKEN IN MUSTARD-CREAM SAUCE 32

PER SERVING: 359 calories; 19.9 grams fat; 40 grams protein; 1.2 grams carbohydrates; 0.3 gram fiber

SAUTÉED MUSHROOMS 46

PER SERVING: 61 calories;
2.5 grams fat; 2.2 grams protein;
9.6 grams carbohydrates;
1.7 grams fiber

SAUTÉED MUSHROOMS
WITH THYME 249

PER SERVING: 35 calories;
1.7 grams fat; 2.2 grams protein;
3.5 grams carbohydrates;
0.9 gram fiber

SAUTÉED SPINACH WITH
GOLDEN RAISINS 276

PER SERVING: 91 calories;
2 grams fat; 6.8 grams protein;
16.1 grams carbohydrates;
6.5 grams fiber

SAUTÉED ZUCCHINI, PEPPERS,
AND TOMATOES 171

PER SERVING: 121 calories;
7.4 grams fat; 3 grams protein;
13.6 grams carbohydrates;
2.9 grams fiber

SESAME CARROT SALAD 62

PER SERVING: 107 calories;
5.8 grams fat; 2.1 grams protein;
12.7 grams carbohydrates;
3.7 grams fiber

SHREDDED BEET AND CARROT
SALAD 193

PER SERVING: 81 calories;
2.6 grams fat; 1.7 grams protein;
14 grams carbohydrates;
3.2 grams fiber

SHRIMP GAZPACHO 103

PER SERVING: 212 calories;
6.6 grams fat; 24.9 grams protein;
12.6 grams carbohydrates;
1.8 grams fiber

SHRIMP PAD THAI 65

PER SERVING: 436 calories;
16.7 grams fat; 23.7 grams protein;
50.2 grams carbohydrates;
2.7 grams fiber

SHRIMP, TOMATO, AND
BASIL PASTA 157

PER SERVING: 483 calories;
10.8 grams fat; 44 grams protein;
52.2 grams carbohydrates;
2.9 grams fiber

SKIRT STEAK WITH
POBLANO SAUCE 134

PER SERVING: 302 calories;
17 grams fat; 28.1 grams protein;
8.8 grams carbohydrates;
1.4 grams fiber

SKIRT STEAK WITH SPICY
GREEN SALSA 128

PER SERVING: 383 calories;
25.4 grams fat; 34.8 grams protein;
2.6 grams carbohydrates;
1.7 grams fiber

SLOPPY JOES 216

PER SERVING: 527 calories;
29.4 grams fat; 26.3 grams protein;
39.4 grams carbohydrates;
3.7 grams fiber

SNAP PEAS WITH MINT 53

PER SERVING: 80 calories;
3.2 grams fat; 3.3 grams protein;
10.3 grams carbohydrates;
3.8 grams fiber

SOLE WITH LEMON-BUTTER
SAUCE 302

PER SERVING: 287 calories;
11 grams fat; 38 grams protein;
5.6 grams carbohydrates;
2 grams fiber

SPAGHETTI CARBONARA 321

PER SERVING: 681 calories;
21.1 grams fat; 32.8 grams protein;
87.2 grams carbohydrates;
2.7 grams fiber

SPAGHETTI WITH
THREE-TOMATO SAUCE 73

PER SERVING: 645 calories;
18.6 grams fat; 18.2 grams protein;
103.2 grams carbohydrates;
6 grams fiber

SPAGHETTI WITH TURKEY
MEATBALLS 326

PER SERVING: 590 calories;
17.1 grams fat; 32.4 grams protein;
75.5 grams carbohydrates;
4.1 grams fiber

SPICY BLACK-BEAN CAKES 310

PER SERVING (WITH LIME SOUR CREAM):
371 calories; 13.9 grams fat;
12.8 grams protein;
48.2 grams carbohydrates;
10.3 grams fiber

SPICY GREEN SALSA 128

PER TABLESPOON SERVING: 68 calories;
7.6 grams fat; 0.1 grams protein;
0.1 grams carbohydrates;
0.1 gram fiber

SPINACH PENNE WITH RICOTTA
AND PINE NUTS 77

PER SERVING: 489 calories;
13.7 grams fat; 20.6 grams protein;
73.2 grams carbohydrates;
15 grams fiber

SPINACH SALAD WITH DRIED
CHERRIES 24

PER SERVING: 201 calories;
11.1 grams fat; 4.8 grams protein;
22.4 grams carbohydrates;
4.8 grams fiber

SPINACH WITH ORZO AND
FETA 85

PER SERVING: 329 calories;
8.8 grams fat; 15.6 grams protein;
50.4 grams carbohydrates;
7.2 grams fiber

SPRING RISOTTO WITH PEAS
AND ZUCCHINI 70

PER SERVING: 347 calories;
7.9 grams fat; 10.7 grams protein;
52.2 grams carbohydrates;
3.1 grams fiber

STEAK AND ONION
SANDWICHES 219

PER SERVING: 412 calories;
26.1 grams fat; 22.7 grams protein;
29.8 grams carbohydrates;
2.4 grams fiber

STEAK WITH PARSLEY SAUCE AND SAUTÉED MUSHROOMS 46

PER SERVING: 481 calories; 36.5 grams fat; 35.3 grams protein; 0.6 gram carbohydrates; 0.3 gram fiber

STEAMED ZUCCHINI WITH SCALLIONS 57

PER SERVING: 55 calories; 3.6 grams fat; 2 grams protein; 5.2 grams carbohydrates; 0.9 gram fiber

STRAWBERRY SHORTCAKES 86

PER SERVING: 473 calories; 24 grams fat; 6.3 grams protein; 59.4 grams carbohydrates; 2.8 grams fiber

SUMMER SNOWBALLS 172

PER SERVING: 451 calories; 28.9 grams fat; 6.3 grams protein; 46.1 grams carbohydrates; 2.5 grams fiber

SWISS CHARD WITH TOASTED BREADCRUMBS 249

PER SERVING: 84 calories; 5.3 grams fat; 3.1 grams protein; 8 grams carbohydrates; 2.4 grams fiber

TANDOORI CHICKEN WITH YOGURT SAUCE 289

PER SERVING (WITHOUT RICE): 346 calories; 6.9 grams fat; 54.5 grams protein; 14.1 grams carbohydrates; 1.6 grams fiber

THAI-STYLE STEAK SALAD 50

PER SERVING: 476 calories; 36.3 grams fat; 23.2 grams protein; 16.7 grams carbohydrates; 5.9 grams fiber

TOMATO AND GRILLED BREAD SALAD 108

PER SERVING: 383 calories; 22.9 grams fat; 7 grams protein; 39.5 grams carbohydrates; 4.6 grams fiber

TOMATO AND OLIVE PENNE 244

PER SERVING: 618 calories; 20.1 grams fat; 17.4 grams protein; 91 grams carbohydrates; 4.2 grams fiber

TORTILLA AND BLACK BEAN PIE 236

PER SERVING: 448 calories; 18.5 grams fat; 20.3 grams protein; 51.8 grams carbohydrates; 7.1 grams fiber

TORTILLA SOUP 19

PER SERVING: 604 calories; 36.3 grams fat; 46.6 grams protein; 23.9 grams carbohydrates; 3.6 grams fiber

TOSSED RADICCHIO AND ENDIVE 329

PER SERVING: 134 calories; 7.4 grams fat (1.1 grams saturated fat); 4.1 grams protein; 15.9 grams carbohydrates; 8.5 grams fiber

TOSTADAS SALSA VERDE 211

PER SERVING: 388 calories; 15.1 grams fat; 35.7 grams protein; 24 grams carbohydrates; 2.8 grams fiber

TURKEY COBB SALAD 36

PER SERVING: 352 calories; 24.4 grams fat; 24.3 grams protein; 11.2 grams carbohydrates; 2.6 grams fiber

VIETNAMESE STEAK SANDWICHES 133

PER SERVING: 569 calories; 14.7 grams fat; 32.1 grams protein; 75.2 grams carbohydrates; 5.1 grams fiber

WARM QUINOA, SPINACH, AND SHIITAKE SALAD 235

PER SERVING: 653 calories; 34 grams fat; 24.8 grams protein; 70 grams carbohydrates; 12.5 grams fiber

WARM WHITE BEAN SALAD 85

PER SERVING: 147 calories; 3.8 grams fat; 6.3 grams protein; 23.3 grams carbohydrates; 5.4 grams fiber

WATERCRESS, ENDIVE, AND GRILLED PEACH SALAD 111

PER SERVING: 279 calories; 19.2 grams fat; 15.7 gram protein; 17.1 grams carbohydrates; 9.3 grams fiber

WHIPPED CREAM 363

PER 1/4 CUP SERVING: 112 calories; 11 grams fat; 0.6 grams protein; 3.2 grams carbohydrates; 0 gram fiber

WHOLE-WHEAT PASTA WITH ROASTED EGGPLANT AND TOMATOES 240

PER SERVING: 370 calories; 14.9 grams fat; 13.2 grams protein; 49.6 grams carbohydrates; 11.5 grams fiber

WILTED SPINACH WITH NUTMEG 224

PER SERVING: 109 calories; 5.7 grams fat; 3.4 grams protein; 15.1 grams carbohydrates; 6.7 grams fiber

ZUCCHINI AND CHICKEN SALAD 115

PER SERVING: 497 calories; 33.5 grams fat; 37.9 gram protein; 13.7 grams carbohydrates; 3.1 grams fiber

ACKNOWLEDGMENTS

This book represents the hard work and dedication of so many talented individuals, on both the book and magazine sides of MSLO. We are grateful to everyone who has been so instrumental in creating our award-winning magazine, especially the team of food editors led by Sandra Rose Gluck. Under Sandy's direction, the team consistently develops the best easy-to-follow recipes for the most delicious dishes, with ingredients that can be found in any supermarket. These creative cooks include Deputy Food Editor Allison Lewis, Senior Associate Food Editor Kristen Evans, and Associate Food Editor Charlyne Mattox. Susan Hanemann and Abigail Chipley also contributed recipes that appear in this book. Assistant Food Editor Kirk C. Hunter provided invaluable help with nutritional analyses.

Scot Schy, the very talented Design and Style Director of *Every Day Food*, created the winning look of the magazine when it launched, and he continues to delight us with each new issue. William van Roden was Art Director of the magazine before stepping up to oversee the design of books and special projects for MSLO. With this book, Will has taken existing material and given it a fresh look, in a new context and format that should appeal to longtime fans of the magazine and new readers alike. Thank you to Matt Papa for his design assistance with this book. We are also grateful to Deputy Art Director Alberto Capolino for his countless contributions to the magazine's design. A big thank you to food stylists Susie Theodorou and Cyd Raftus MacDowell for making our recipes look mouthwatering, and for being such a pleasure to work with.

Ellen Morrissey, Executive Book Editor, worked with the magazine editors and designers to select the recipes and compile them into a cohesive whole. She was ably assisted by Christine Cyr. Amy Conway, Editor in Chief of Special Projects, and Associate Managing Editor Christiane Angeli provided editorial input and guidance at various points throughout the book project.

As always, we are grateful to Editorial Director Margaret Roach and Creative Director Eric A. Pike for their guidance and creative input with this and all our publications, and to Chief Creative Officer Gael Towey and President of Publishing Lauren Podlach Stanich for their continued leadership.

Many thanks to our friends at Clarkson Potter and Crown Publishers, including President Jenny Frost, Publisher Lauren Shakely, Editorial Director Doris Cooper, Marketing Director Sydney Webber, and the design, managing editorial, and production teams, including Jane Treuhaft, Marysarah Quinn, Mark McCauslin, Amy Boorstein, Linnea Knollmueller, and Derek Gullino.

Finally, a great big thanks to our loyal readers and customers, who have been so supportive of our efforts with this "little" magazine from the beginning, and who remind us every day of the importance of putting good, healthy, straightforward meals on the table for our families.

CREDITS

LISA COHEN
52, 67, 79, 82, top right & bottom left, 84 top right, 87, 306, 307, 315, 316, 328 bottom right, 356, 357, 362, 363

CHRIS COURT
47, 82 top left & bottom right, 92, 93, 129–132, 139, 144, 151, 152, 248 bottom left, 254, 255, 262, 268, 269, 294, 302, 303, 319, 338, 360

JOHN KERNICK
22, 23, 44, 45, 63, 104, 105, 117, 124, 125, 148, 155, 166–169, 170 top right, 191, 203, 206, 207, 225, 246 top left, 258, 259, 273, 346, 361

DAVID LOFTUS
26, 55, 64, 75, 80, 181, 187, 192, 199, 214, 222, 238, 248 top right, 250, 264, 265, 278, 292, 311, 324, 328 top right

JONATHAN LOVEKIN
5, 6, 16, 17, 48, 49, 50, 51, 59

WILLIAM MEPPEM
84 bottom right, 173, 178, 226, 334

MINH + WASS
18, 21, 29, 30, 33, 34, 38, 42, 56, 60, 68, 71, 84 top left & bottom left, 88, 95, 184, 200, 277, 282, 291, 327, 330 top left & bottom right, 333, 337, 343, 348, 349

AMY NEUNSINGER
101, 170 bottom left, 234, 320, 321, 344

CON POULOS
37, 41, 72, 76, 91, 188, 195, 204, 209, 221, 237, 245, 246 bottom right, 248 top left & bottom right, 257, 270, 271, 300, 304, 323, 340, 341, 358

JOSÉ MANUEL PICAYO RIVERA
14, 96, 118, 136, 137, 156, 157, 160, 161, 176, 177, 182, 210, 260, 296, 297, 308, 309, 350, 351

KIRSTEN STRECKER
24, 25, 328 top left & bottom left

CLIVE STREETER
98, 102, 106, 109, 110, 113, 114, 121, 122, 126, 135, 140, 143, 147, 159, 163, 164, 170 top left & bottom right, 174, 196, 213, 217, 218, 229, 230, 242, 246 bottom left, 253, 274, 281, 286, 288, 289, 298, 299, 312, 330 top right & bottom left, 352–353, 354, 359

MIKKEL VANG
233, 241, 246 top right, 266, 285

INDEX